358.403   c.1

WINTON.
   AIR POWER AT SEA.

1987   1990 27.95   10-87
1989

AIR
POWER
AT SEA

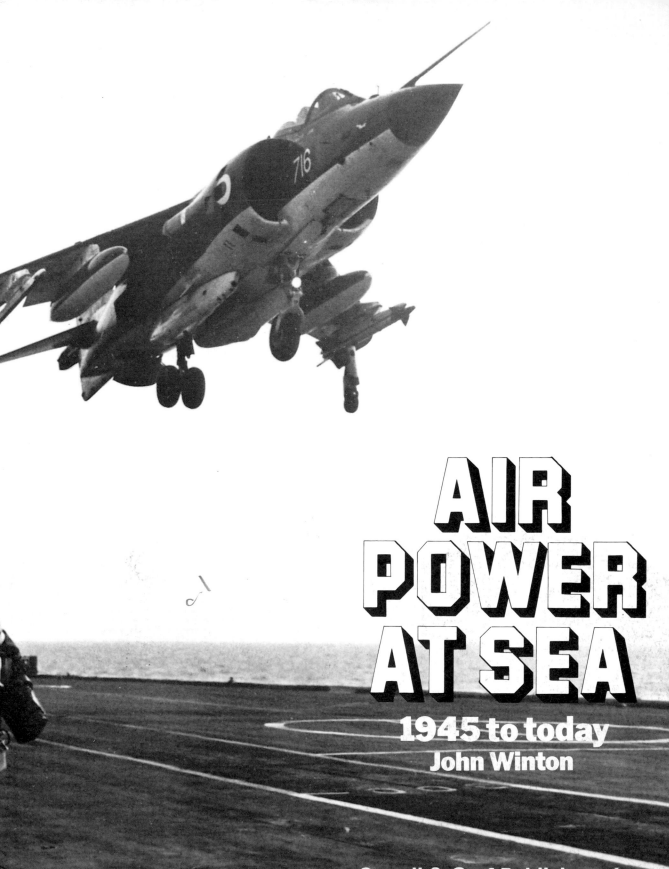

AIR POWER AT SEA

1945 to today
John Winton

Carroll & Graf Publishers, Inc
New York

Page 1: US Navy SH–3A helicopter delivering
mail to a US destroyer in the Gulf of Tonkin,
January 1968. Title pages: Sea Harrier of 800
Squadron landing on HMS *Hermes* on her way to
the Falklands, April 1982

Copyright © 1987 by John Winton
First published in Great Britain by
Sidgwick & Jackson Ltd Publishers 1987
First Carroll & Graf edition 1987

Carroll & Graf Publishers, Inc
260 Fifth Avenue
New York, NY 10001

Library of Congress Cataloging-in-Publication Data

Winton, John.
   Air power at sea.

   Includes index
   1. Naval aviation.   2. Military history, Modern–
20th century.   I. Title.
VG90.W56   1987   358.4'03   87–15790

ISBN: 0–88184–358–X

Manufactured in Great Britain

Contents

Tokyo Bay, 2 September 1945.
The surrender of Japan on the
USS *Missouri*

After the War Was Over

'LET us pray that peace be now restored to the world and that God will preserve it always,' said General MacArthur. 'These proceedings are now closed.' It was 2 September 1945. MacArthur had just accepted the surrender of Japan during a strangely subdued and anti-climactic ceremony when, as Admiral Sir Bruce Fraser, who signed on behalf of the United Kingdom, noticed, 'the silence was complete except for the whirring and clicking of cameras, and one could feel that all present at that gathering were struggling to adjust themselves to the fact that they were witnessing the act which put an end to a long and bitter war'.

That ceremony took place on the deck of the battleship USS *Missouri*, at anchor in Tokyo Bay. But, on the balance of achievement at sea, against Japan and against Germany, it should have been held on the flight deck of an aircraft carrier. At that moment, whilst various dignitaries were signing, aircraft carriers of the US Third Fleet, which then included one British carrier, HMS *Indefatigable*, were still at sea, to guard against last-minute treachery. Naval and Marine aircraft had also begun flights over the Japanese mainland to discover the whereabouts of POW and internee camps still unknown.

In six years of war at sea, aircraft had distinguished themselves from the North Atlantic to the South Pacific and from the Arctic to the Indian Ocean. They had sunk or disabled a long line of noble capital ships, at Taranto, at Pearl Harbor, in the South China Sea, in Norway, off Leyte Gulf, off Okinawa and in the home harbours of Japan. Aircraft were just as deadly to their own kind, in the Coral Sea, at Midway and again at Leyte Gulf.

Enemy aircraft had sunk 820 Allied merchant ships, amounting to nearly three million tons of shipping. Aircraft had sunk 306 German U-boats and shared 48 more with surface ships. Bombing raids destroyed a further 62 U-boats. Naval and Marine aircraft had sunk 174 Japanese ships.

For the carriers, the first task after the Japanese surrender was humanitarian. There were an estimated 125,000 POWs and internees in some 250 camps known to the International Red Cross stretching across the Far East from Java to Japan and from Burma to Manchuria. The fleets were the only immediately practical means of repatriating these men and women. Of those repatriated, the great majority went home by sea.

The American aircraft carriers played their part in Operation MAGIC CARPET, in which more than two million men and women were ferried back to the United States. Some 400,000 Japanese, Chinese and Korean soldiers were eventually returned to their homelands.

For the British carriers, the work of repatriation began while the fleet was still in Tokyo Bay. The escort carrier HMS *Speaker* left Tokyo Bay on 3 September amidst some emotional scenes. Her Commanding Officer, Captain U.H.R. James, took his ship to sea 'by a most circuitous route' so as to pass as many ships as possible.

'As she steamed through the British anchorage,' wrote one eye-witness, 'the ship's companies of all the British ships gave her a send-off which those who saw it will never forget. The sight of this small carrier with her ship's company fallen in for leaving harbour in accordance with naval custom but with in addition these hundreds of ex-prisoners of war ranged on her flight-deck, cheering like mad and being cheered, brought tears to the eyes and the realisation of what the presence of the great Fleet in Tokyo Bay meant to these men.'

On 13 September, another escort carrier, HMS *Ruler*, sailed with 445 passengers who 'ranged from senior Colonels to Chinese babies and included African negroes, Baptist missionaries, Indian school-teachers and a number of miscellaneous Asiatics'. The hangar had been converted into a vast dormitory which, according to one lady, 'looked like a fairy land' – 'a description', her Captain commented, 'which had not previously been heard in this ship'. Final proof that the war really was over came at six o'clock on the first evening at sea, with the pipe 'Children to supper'.

Massed Allied aircraft flying over the battleship HMS *Duke of York*, Admiral Fraser's flagship, after the signing of the Japanese surrender

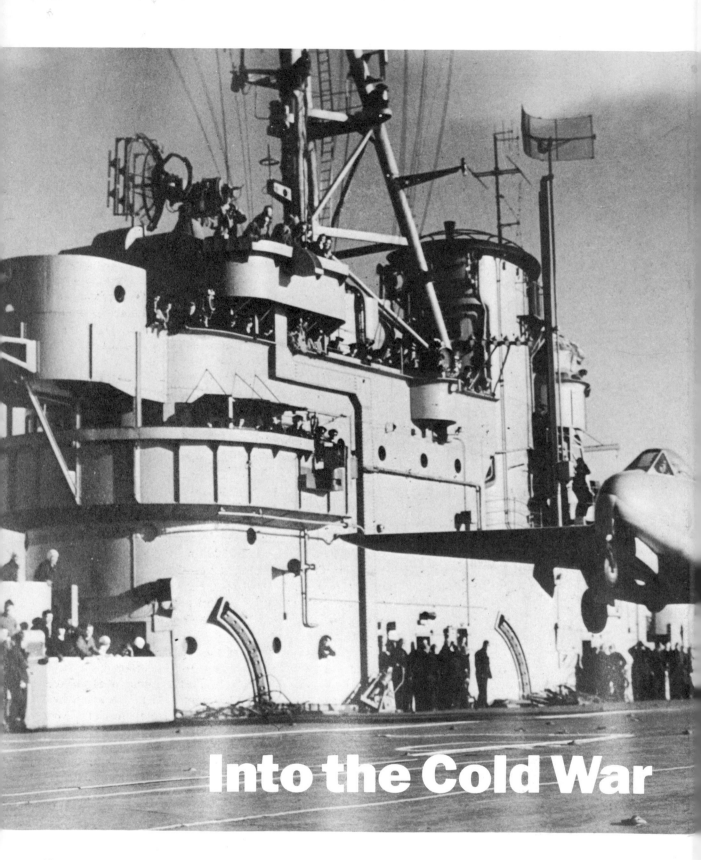

Into the Cold War

Sea Vampire trials on board
HMS *Ocean*, 3 December 1945

AT the end of the war, only the Royal Navy and the United States Navy had naval air power. The German *Graf Zeppelin* and the Italian *Aquila* never saw service and of Japan's twenty-five carriers nineteen had been sunk, two had foundered in harbour after air attacks, and all the rest were damaged, some almost completely wrecked.

The US Navy had itself lost twelve carriers during the war but in July 1945 still had twenty-six, either in commission or building, of the 27,000 ton, 33 knot, 100-aircraft *Essex* class carriers which had formed the backbone of the Fast Carrier Task Forces of the Pacific war. But the US Navy also had eight light carriers of the 11,000 ton, 31 knot, 30-aircraft *Independence* class and seventy escort carriers (CVEs), with a total naval aircraft strength of about 41,000, of all types. By 1 July 1946, the US Navy had twelve *Essex* class, one remaining *Independence* class, and ten CVEs. But the first two of a new giant 45,000 ton 120-aircraft, *Midway* and *Franklin D. Roosevelt*, commissioned in 1945. Their design incorporated the lessons of the carrier war just ended, having armoured flight decks and much greater compartmentation, to minimize the effect of action damage.

Lend-lease ended as soon as the war ended. For the Fleet Air Arm, all US aircraft had to be returned at once, or paid for. In practice, the majority of them were ditched. Carriers steamed out to sea beyond Sydney Heads, their flight decks crammed with F4U Corsair fighter-bombers and Avenger TBRs which were simply pushed over the side. Over 700 aircraft were finally disposed of, in one way or another.

For the Royal Navy, this unceremonious dumping of aircraft was only the beginning of a long process of reduction. The wartime carrier building programme was drastically cut. Three projected 45,000 ton carriers, *Gibraltar, Malta, New Zealand*, never left the drawing board. Of four planned 34,000 ton *Audacious* class, only two were built: *Audacious* herself, renamed *Eagle*, commissioned in 1951, and *Irresistible* (as *Ark Royal*) in 1955. A class of eight 13,800 ton *Hermes* class carriers was cut to four: *Centaur, Albion* and *Bulwark*, commissioned in 1954 and 1955, and *Hermes* herself (though not until 1959).

There were also sixteen ships of the 14,000 ton *Colossus* and *Majestic* classes, which were to have varied histories. *Glory, Vengeance* and *Venerable* were just in time for operational service in the war, and *Ocean, Theseus* and *Triumph* in later years. Several of these carriers were eventually sold to foreign navies. Two, *Perseus* and *Pioneer*, were completed as aircraft maintenance ships. The thirty-five American-built and four British-built escort carriers, which had done such yeoman service providing air cover for convoys and assault landings, were all quickly returned to merchant service.

The Royal Navy's main carrier strength in 1945 was in the six fleet carriers *Illustrious, Victorious, Formidable, Indomitable*,

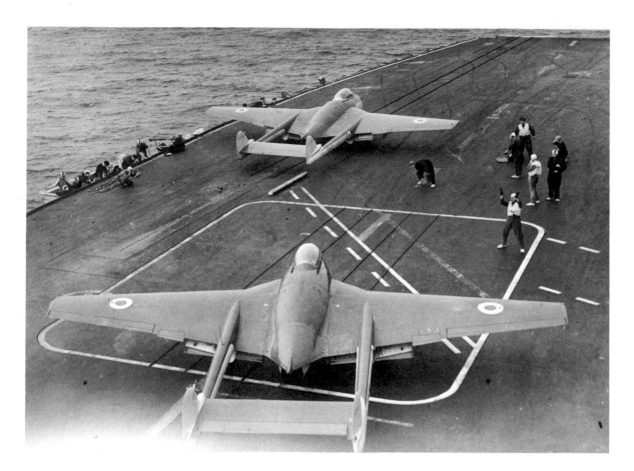

Vampires of No. 1832 RNVR
Squadron on board HMS
Theseus, June 1950

Indefatigable and *Implacable*. Although they had all seen hectic wartime service (especially *Illustrious*) they were hardly used operationally after the war, being employed for the most part as trials and training ships, until *Victorious* finally emerged after much modernization in the 1960s.

In 1945 there were no operational jet aircraft at sea but the shape of future aircraft had been shown in the skies over wartime Germany with the appearance in December 1944 of the marvellous Messerschmitt Me.262, the world's first operational jet fighter, with a speed of 540 mph at 20,000 feet, which had carved through the P.51 Mustang fighter screens around the B.17 Flying Fortress formation as though they were butter.

On 6 November 1945, an experimental Ryan Fireball XFR–1 piston-jet aircraft made an emergency landing on USS *Wake Island* after its piston engine had failed. But the first controlled landing by a true jet aircraft was made on 3 December 1945, off the Isle of Wight, when Lieutenant Commander Eric ('Winkle') Brown landed a Vampire I on the flight deck of HMS *Ocean*. For such an historic occasion, it was almost an anti-climax: 'I settled down on my final approach to the deck,' said Brown, 'and immediately realised that the ship was moving much more violently than I had thought before, pitching and rolling. But my Vampire was so steady in her approach descent and the batsman was giving me such a steady signal that it never even crossed my mind that I might have to go round again. I came straight in and made a very gentle landing, although camera shots showed that the pitching stern had hit my tail booms just before I touched down.'

Two days of trials, with fifteen take-offs and landings, convinced the high-ranking spectators embarked that jet flying was feasible. 'The shortness of our take-off run astonished all the goofers on the island. We soared past them at captain's eye level, twenty feet up.'

Although the Vampire was an excellent deck-landing aircraft, with no propeller torque and a good view forward over the nose, it was slow to accelerate and had a low endurance and it never entered squadron service. The Royal Navy's first operational jet fighter was the 590 mph Supermarine Attacker which started carrier trials in 1947. 800 Squadron were equipped with Attacker F.1s in August 1951. But by then the US Navy had the 540 mph North American Fury FJ-1, in service by 1948, followed a year later by the 600 mph McDonnell F2H Banshee. In the same year the US Navy began to operate the 466 mph two-engined North American Savage bomber, the first naval aircraft capable of carrying and delivering the atomic bomb.

The atomic bombs dropped on Hiroshima and Nagasaki and the later test detonations at Bikini Atoll overshadowed everything and seemed to make all previous naval tactics obsolete. Strategists, and politicians especially, were tempted to pin their faith, the nation's money and the armed services' weapon delivery systems on the bomb and neglect or deride everything else. But the international scene was darkening with events in which the bomb was irrelevant. In 1948 an elected government in Czechoslovakia was overturned by a communist coup and Czechoslovakia went behind the Iron Curtain. In June that year the Soviets blockaded Berlin by land and the Berlin Airlift began. In 1949, the Chinese Communists achieved victory on the mainland over the Nationalists. British warships had been fired on frequently during the conflict. The frigate HMS *Amethyst*, trapped in the Yangtse river, extricated herself and reached the open sea in a daring escape which thrilled the Western world. In none of these circumstances did the atomic bomb have any direct relevance or effect.

In the United States, there was a strong move towards unification of the armed services, to achieve better co-ordination and economy of expense. The US Army Air Force favoured it as a likely means of gaining independence from the US Army. The Army also favoured it, as a possible means of absorbing the US Marine Corps. The US Navy saw it as a threat, which could deprive them of their essential air arm. However, the National Security Act of 1947 created three services, Navy, Army and Air Force, which ensured that the Navy survived as a 'multi-faceted service' with its own integral air power.

Attackers FB.2s of 800
Squadron on board HMS *Eagle*,
1952

But this was not by any means the end of the debate or of inter-
service rivalry. The newly-created Air Force argued that the
atomic bomb overrode every other consideration. The mere threat
of it would prevent future wars. Delivered by the US Air Force, the
bomb would deter aggression with the minimum expenditure of US
dollars and cost in American lives. It was a seductive theory. But
the Navy consistently argued for a more flexible policy. The
country could not anticipate what sort of future war it would be
called upon to fight. Where, when and with what weapons would be
chosen by the aggressor. The United States should therefore never
settle for a fixed concept of how a war was going to be fought. The
country should be prepared to fight many different types of war in
different areas with different weapons. There should never be
preconceived restrictions on ideas or on weapons.

Air power, deployed worldwide, was the key. The Navy's duty
was to be able to project air power to gain control of the air and
with it the sea on a worldwide scale. As an example, in 1947 the US
Navy stationed an aircraft carrier permanently in the Mediterranean – this being the birth of the Sixth Fleet.

The whole debate took place in a heated atmosphere of recrimi-
nation and accusation, with highly partisan speeches in the House

and Senate and inflammatory articles in newspapers and magazines. On 18 April 1949, the keel of a new aircraft carrier, to be named *United States*, was laid at Newport News, Virginia. But five days later, the carrier was cancelled by the Secretary of Defense, Louis A. Johnson, without the knowledge or approval of the Secretary for the Navy, John L. Sullivan, who was out of Washington at the time and promptly resigned. There were rumours that the Navy's air arm was to be reduced and perhaps even transferred to the USAF, that the Marines were to be abolished entirely and their air arm also merged into the USAF, while the Navy was to become merely a convoy and escort force, with some submarines.

The argument might have gone on interminably, but suddenly and quite unexpectedly the Navy's case was made in the most forceful and convincing manner.

To General MacArthur, Supreme Commander, Occupied Japan, the news came like another Pearl Harbor. 'I had an uncanny feeling of nightmare,' he wrote. 'It had been nine years before, on a Sunday morning, at the same hour, that a telephone call with the same note of urgency had awakened me in the penthouse atop the Manila Hotel.'

Korea

T HE news was that at 4 am that Sunday, 25 June 1950, after a forty-five-minute bombardment, six divisions of the North Korean People's Army, with artillery and 100 Soviet-made T34 and T70 tanks, had crossed the 38th Parallel and were advancing into South Korea. The attacking force, initially some 100,000 troops, was reinforced by two more divisions on 26 June, and by the 28th the North Koreans were in the South Korean capital of Seoul. Another 10,000 troops landed at Kangnung and Samchok, on the east coast. Meanwhile, the South Korean Army, caught utterly by surprise, unprepared and ill-equipped, retreated in disorder.

The Korean peninsula had been effectively partitioned since the end of the war, when occupying Japanese troops surrendered to the Russians north of the 38th Parallel and to the Americans in the south. The 38th Parallel was intended (certainly so far as the Americans were concerned) as an arbitrary dividing line with no permanent political significance. But over the years the Soviets and the North Koreans had made of the parallel a true frontier, a boundary between two ideologies. By 1950 there were two *de facto* governments in Korea, in the north supported by Soviet Russia, in the south by the United States, both claiming sovereignty over the whole peninsula.

Encouraged by recent pronouncements that South Korea was outside the American defence perimeter, Soviet Russia believed that the United States and United Nations neither could nor would resist an invasion of South Korea. In fact, United States and United Nations reaction was, for the Soviets, disconcertingly swift. By 2 July, after United Nations resolutions condemning the invasion and the appointment of MacArthur in operational command, British and American warships of Task Force 77, representing the United Nations, were already off the coast of Korea. At dawn on that day, in the first naval action of the Korean war, the cruiser HMS *Jamaica* and the sloop HMS *Black Swan* engaged six North Korean E-boats and sank five of them.

Air strikes, the first of many thousands flown in the next three years, began at dawn the next day. At 0545 on 3 July, the carrier HMS *Triumph*, in the Yellow Sea off the coast of Korea, launched twelve Firefly fighter-bombers of 827 Squadron and nine rocket-armed Seafire 47s of 800 Squadron to attack hangars and installations at Haeju airfield, with railways and bridges as secondary targets. The aircraft all returned safely, though some had minor flak damage.

At 0600 USS *Valley Forge* launched sixteen F4U Corsairs of VF–54, each armed with eight 5 inch rockets, and twelve Skyraiders of VF–55 armed with two 500 lb and six 100 lb bombs, to attack the airfield at Pyongyang, the capital of North Korea. Eight F9F2 Panthers, led by the air group commander, Commander Harvey P. Lanham, were catapulted shortly afterwards, to overtake the strike and give air cover. These were the first jet fighters used in combat by the US Navy.

There were further sorties from both carriers that afternoon and
on the following day, 4 July. At Pyongyang, aircraft were
destroyed on the ground, and three hangars were demolished.
Elsewhere in the city, road and rail bridges, locomotives and
rolling stock, various installations and buildings were bombed,
rocketed and strafed with cannon shells. Four Skyraiders were
slightly damaged by flak which was generally scattered and
inaccurate. The greatest damage was done by a returning
Skyraider, unable to lower its flaps, which bounced *Valley Forge*'s
crash barriers and landed in the deck park forward, destroying one
Skyraider and two Corsairs, and badly damaging another three
Skyraiders, one Corsair and two Panthers. But when the carriers
withdrew to refuel on 5 July, they were well satisfied with their
start. Many were reminded of the Third Fleet's strikes over Japan
in 1945. Once again, after a lapse of five years, US and British
aircraft carriers were conducting joint operations over enemy
territory.

Wonsan oil refinery during the
attack by US Navy aircraft,
18 July 1950

Despite support from the sea, the South Koreans continued to be
driven back. American troops were hastily flown in, and many
more were to arrive by sea. But meanwhile the United Nations
front retreated steadily. On 15 July North Korean troops reached
the city of Taejon. On the same day, the US First Cavalry Division
made an amphibious landing at Pohang on the east coast, for
which *Valley Forge* (proving the flexibility of naval air power)
provided air cover. This anchored the eastern end of the front, but
the North Koreans continued to advance and by 24 July had
reached Mokpo, in the south of the peninsula.

On 18 July *Valley Forge* launched a major strike against the

Wonsan oil refinery with eleven AD Skyraiders, each carrying a 1,000 lb bomb, a 500 lb bomb and rockets, and ten F4U Corsairs armed with two rockets each and full belts of 20 mm ammunition. The Corsairs dived over the target, which 'stood out like a sore thumb', from 4,000 feet firing their rockets in pairs. The Skyraiders followed them down to plaster the refinery area with bombs and rockets. 'When the attack was finished,' reported the Corsair leader, 'it was difficult to see the target or to distinguish portions of the plant that were not destroyed due to the tremendous clouds of belching smoke from the refinery . . . There were constant explosions as the fires steadily spread to the unbombed areas. The entire coast appeared to be on fire.'

It was already clear that sea power was the only way of holding the ring in Korea, to bring in reinforcements and supplies for the beleaguered Eighth Army which was being compressed into a restricted defensive perimeter extending only a few miles around the southern port of Pusan. On 23 July another carrier, USS *Boxer*, arrived from the United States with 145 P.51 Mustang fighters for the Far Eastern Air Force, having steamed across the Pacific in just over eight days.

As the Army continued to fall back, the carriers received more and more urgent calls for close air support. The Navy system of close air support was developed by the US Marines in pre-war actions in Nicaragua, Haiti and Santo Domingo, when aircraft and infantry operated together for the first time, and refined during the Second World War at Tarawa, Iwo Jima and especially in Okinawa. The front-line commander had aircraft allocated to him, for his own use, and had with him an air liaison officer to assist him to select targets and to transmit instructions and information to the aircraft orbiting overhead, calling down strikes as required. 'Close' in this context meant targets within 200 or even 50 yards. The Air Force system developed in the European theatre of the Second World War, relied upon airborne controllers circling the front-line area in light liaison-type aircraft. Missions were centrally controlled. Strike aircraft would be assigned a particular mission and receive their instructions from the airborne controller when they arrived over the target area. 'Close support' under this system meant anything up to ten miles from the front.

Valley Forge began close support on 25 and 26 July but her pilots soon began to experience difficulties in establishing communications with the airborne controllers. Many pilots spent some time circling around, trying to report their presence. Some gave up and flew away to find targets of opportunity on their own. First attempts at liaison were close to chaotic. Proper maps were lacking; the Air Force were using one type, the Navy another. The radio channels in the controllers' 'Mosquito planes' were overloaded. Voice procedure discipline was nonexistent, resulting in incomprehensible babble.

Meanwhile, F80 Shooting Stars were arriving from Japan and having to be used at once because of fuel endurance they could only spend some five minutes over the target area. Thus, Navy aircraft 'bristling' with bombs and rockets had to stand aside and wait whilst lightly loaded USAF Shooting Stars were called in for strikes. HMS *Truimph* had been having reliability, and suitability, problems with her aircraft and especially her Seafires, with their very short endurance. Her air group therefore concentrated upon flying combat air patrols (CAPs) over the ships, so as to allow every possible aircraft from *Valley Forge* free to fly over the mainland.

On 1 August, USS *Philippine Sea* arrived with Carrier Air Group 11, with two squadrons (VF–111 and 112) of Panthers, two squadrons (VF–113 and 114) of Corsairs, and one squadron (VA–115) of AD Skyraiders. She was badly needed. By 8 August the situation on the ground had deteriorated to the point where it was thought the entire front might collapse and Eighth Army would be overwhelmed. *Valley Forge* and *Philippine Sea* therefore redoubled their close air support, flying for two days at a time, and withdrawing on the third day in order to refuel and re-arm.

While the carriers of Task Force 77 were trying, with mixed success, to carry out close air support according to Air Force doctrine, two escort carriers, USS *Sicily* and *Badoeng Strait*, with two Marine Corsair squadrons VMF–214 and 323 embarked, arrived on 3 August and began, as part of Task Group 96.8, to practise the Marine way of doing it in support of the newly-arrived 1st Provisional Marine Brigade ashore.

The Marines kept six aircraft over their brigade in the Pusan perimeter throughout daylight hours. On one typical day when the Marines were preparing to assault enemy positions at Kaesong, Marine observers spotted a column of almost a hundred enemy vehicles preparing to make a dash for safety. The ground controller called down four Corsairs circling overhead who made an immediate low strafing run. Vehicles collided with one another or ran off the road. Soviet-made jeeps and motorcycles were abandoned. But two of the Corsairs were hit. One crashed in a paddy field, killing the pilot. The pilot of the second Corsair was picked up by a passing helicopter which was carrying the brigade commander. By 14 September, *Sicily*'s Corsairs had flown 688 sorties and *Badoeng Strait*'s 671. The twenty-four aircraft from these two 'jeep' carriers achieved an availability rate of 92 per cent.

Such was the intensity of the flying, from the earliest days in Korea, that in the period from 5 August to 3 September TF 77's carriers had launched over 3,000 strikes. The air strikes from TF 77 and TG 96.8, with gunfire support from warships, played a major part in saving Pusan and stabilizing the front line in a narrow pocket about fifty miles from the city.

Opposite above: F4U–4B Corsair being directed onto the catapult of USS *Philippine Sea* off Korea, 19 October 1950

Below: Night strike on Korea. US Marine F4U Corsair on board USS *Sicily*, 16 September 1950

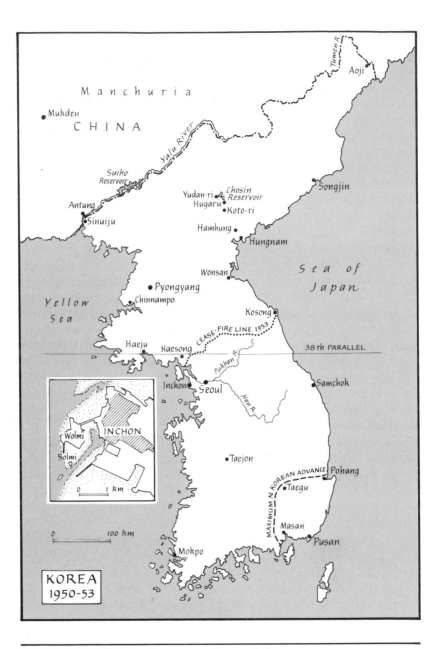

Map labels:

Manchuria

CHINA

• Mukden

Yalu River

Suiho Reservoir

Antung

Sinuiju

Yudan-ri

Chosin Reservoir

Hugaru

• Koto-ri

Hamhung

Hungnam

Songjin

Aoji

Tumen R.

Sea of Japan

Wonsan

• Pyongyang

Chinnampo

Yellow Sea

Kosong

CEASE-FIRE LINE 1953

Haeju

Kaesong

Pukhan R.

38th PARALLEL

Inchon

Seoul

Han R.

Samchok

INCHON (inset)

Wolmi

Solmi

0   1 km

• Taejon

MAXIMUM N. KOREAN ADVANCE

Pohang

• Taegu

Masan

• Pusan

0   100 km

• Mokpo

KOREA 1950-53

Inchon – The Great Gamble

It was in late August 1950, when the United Nations forces had been compressed into the small bridgehead around Pusan and things were looking their blackest, that MacArthur himself had the idea of a landing somewhere up on the west coast of Korea, well behind the front line. The choice of landing place was critical. Too far to the north, near Pyongyang, for example, would overstretch the available forces – and the luck. Too near, and the North Koreans would simply be able to withdraw and regroup to the north of the landing.

Inchon seemed perfect. It had a large harbour. It was only fifteen miles from Seoul, through which the main North Korean supply route to the south now ran. An Inchon landing would cut the North Korean supply route, shorten the war, and save casualties. It could well make a campaign in the bitter Korean winter weather unnecessary. Another point (seldom spoken out loud) was that a successful amphibious landing would not only shorten the war – it would save the Marines.

As events proved, the North Koreans would never have expected an assault landing at Inchon. In fact they would have regarded the idea as insane. Inchon had a tidal range of some 33 feet, one of the greatest in the Far East. There were currents running at five to six knots. Acres of mudbanks dried out at low tide. The main approach, Flying Fish Channel, was narrow and tortuous, a difficult pilotage passage even in peacetime and in daylight. Inchon was a major city, with more than a quarter of a million inhabitants. The Marines would have to make an assault landing across sea walls in downtown Inchon. The landing ships carrying the assault troops and their guns and armour needed 29 feet of water under their keels and therefore, because of the tidal conditions at Inchon, the landings could only be made on three or four days a month. By simply looking at tide-tables the defenders could make a good estimate of the day, and even the time, of a landing. 'We drew up a list of every conceivable and natural handicap,' said one gunfire support officer, 'and Inchon had 'em all.' The best the Navy would say about Inchon was that 'it was not impossible'. MacArthur himself called it a 5,000–1 gamble.

The tides decided that the landing had to be on or around 15 September, 11 October, or 3 November. The earliest date, 15 September, was chosen, and planning was completed in twenty-three days. The basic plan was: neutralize the islands of Wolmi-Do and Solmi-Do, guarding the approach; land and invade Inchon; seize the major airfield at Kimpo; go on to capture Seoul.

The preliminaries began on 10 September when Marine Corsairs from USS *Sicily* and *Badoeng Strait* strafed Wolmi and Solmi and burned them out with napalm. On the 13th the pre-invasion bombardment began, with four cruisers, USS *Toledo* and *Rochester* and HMS *Kenya* and *Jamaica*, and six US destroyers bombarding the islands, while TF 77 Corsairs struck from the air. After three days of bombardment, Marines landed on Wolmi-Do early on the morning of 15 September and took the island in forty-two minutes.

The main landing went in at 1730 the same day, after a final forty-five-minute bombardment of the assualt beaches that afternoon by rocket ships, destroyers, cruisers and aircraft. The approaches were not mined (although it transpired that they would have been in a few more weeks). It was just before dusk and the Marines, landing over the sea walls into the heart of the city, had no time to establish themselves in defensive positions against possible counter-attacks during the night. Furthermore, LSTs

(landing ships, tank) with some 3,000 tons of immediately necessary supplies had to follow the Marines in and remain on the mud flats close to shore until the next day.

But all went well. The Marines landed with very little difficulty, against light opposition. The next day they pressed on into the city and by the evening were mopping up the last pockets of resistance. The Marines continued to advance inland, took the important airfield at Kimpo at 9 pm on the 17th and reached Seoul on the 26th. In the first two days the Marines suffered a total of 222 casualties, killed, missing and wounded.

There was very little enemy air activity. At 0550 on the 17th, two North Korean YAK–3 aircraft bombed USS *Rochester*, one of them being shot down by HMS *Jamaica*. Aircraft from the Fast Carrier Task Force (TF 77), which now included three carriers, *Valley Forge*, *Philippine Sea* and *Boxer* (which had joined on 15 September), flew CAPs over the whole area and interdiction strikes on road and rail communications inland. HMS *Triumph*'s aircraft, with the Blockade and Covering Force under Vice Admiral W.G. Andrewes, flew 112 sorties covering 251,000 square miles in the fourteen days up to 30 September.

There was no doubt that the Inchon landing had been brilliantly successful. The 5,000–1 shot had come off. The North Korean Army was shattered and tried desperately to regroup. Many of its units were trapped in the south. On the day of the landing, Eighth Army broke out of the Pusan perimeter and advanced northwards, to join with elements of X Corps south of Seoul on the 26th. Pyongyang was taken on 19 October. It seemed that the war might all be over in a very few weeks.

Inchon had important political benefits for the United States armed forces, and especially for the Navy and the Marines. It proved that the Navy was still a practicable and reliable means of implementing the strategic policies of the USA. It guaranteed the future of the Marine Corps. In a sense Inchon brought defence thinking and planning in all the countries of the West and especially those in NATO out from under the shadow of the nuclear mushroom cloud, by showing that traditional principles of sea and air power, demonstrated over and over again in the Second World War, were by no means obsolete.

The Yalu Bridges

On 9 October, *Triumph* was relieved by a sister ship, HMS *Theseus*, with the 17th Carrier Air Group embarked, of twenty-one Sea Fury FB.IIs of 807 Squadron and twelve Firefly AS.Vs of 810 Squadron. On 10 October, *Theseus*' first day of operations, Lieutenant S. Leonard of 807 Squadron was shot down and his Sea Fury crash-landed behind enemy lines. Leonard himself was badly injured. Despite enemy interference, a USAF helicopter rescued him two hours later. This was one of the first of many such rescues in the

Korean campaign, where the helicopter was to come into its own, ashore and afloat.

There was hardly any opposition at sea, although the North Korean Navy was reported to have some submarines. From the beginning, the North Koreans virtually abdicated control of the sea on both coasts to the United Nations. Thus the carrier aircraft flew their sorties almost entirely against land targets, except for CAPs and anti-submarine patrols over and around their own ships. Their main task, along with the USAF, the South Korean Air Force and units of air forces of other United Nations countries such as Australia, Greece and South Africa, was the prolonged and ultimately unsuccessful attempt to sever the enemy's supply lines – in effect to try and cut off the Korean peninsula along the line of the Yalu and Tumen rivers. Even with the help of a sustained and successful sea blockade of both coasts, and despite quite major local successes achieved over deceptively encouraging periods of time, the task proved to be beyond the capacity of air power.

The carriers' first specific task was the destruction of the bridges over the Yalu river in November 1950. In October, the United Nations had continued a steady advance north towards the Yalu on two quite separate fronts. In the west, Eighth Army under Major General Walton Walker was advancing from Pyongyang, while X Corps under Major General E.M. Almond was pushing up from Hamhung in the east. The two armies were separated both by eighty miles of mountain territory and an apparently unbridgeable mental gulf. There was little communication and almost no common planning or consultation between them.

During October, Chinese troops (described by Peking Radio as 'volunteers') were reported in Korea in growing numbers. By the end of the month, units of four separate Chinese armies had been identified from interrogation of POWs. On 1 November Russian-built MiG fighters appeared over the Yalu and fired on United Nations aircraft. UN aircraft were also fired on by Red anti-aircraft guns sited on the Manchurian side of the border. Reconnaissance showed that communist reinforcements and supplies were crossing into Korea over the seventeen bridges, six of them major ones, across the Yalu.

Bridges, by their very shape and nature, are awkward targets for aerial attack. But the Yalu bridges were made even more difficult by politically-imposed restrictions. UN aircraft were forbidden to fly across the Manchurian border. They could not drop bombs, nor retaliate against anti-aircraft fire from the other side. If attacked in the air they could not follow MiGs across the border, even in hot pursuit. For the B–29 Superfortresses of the Far Eastern Air Force, who made many of the early sorties against the bridges, the task was almost impossible; as they flew down the Yalu towards their targets, the wide and sweeping bends in the river made it virtually inevitable that they would fly over, or even drop some of their bombs on, the Manchurian side. Even the carrier pilots were permitted to attack only the first bridge spans on the Korean side and instead of approaching by the best way, along the length of the bridges, they had to attack at right angles.

The main carrier effort began on 9 November, with strikes by aircraft from *Valley Forge*, *Philippine Sea* and *Leyte* which had

arrived from the Mediterranean on 3 October, having steamed some 18,500 miles at an average speed of 22 knots – yet another example of the flexibility of naval air power. She had embarked CAG 3 with the normal complement of an *Essex* class carrier: two squadrons of Panthers, two of Corsairs, and one of AD Skyraiders. (Operational experience was to show that five squadrons were too cumbersome, and this complement was later reduced to four.)

The strike groups from each carrier consisted of at least twenty-four aircraft and sometimes as many as forty. Each strike normally had eight AD Skyraiders, carrying two 1,000 lb bombs, or occasionally one 2,000 lb bomb, with full belts of 20 mm ammunition. The Corsairs carried eight 5 inch rockets, or eight 100 lb bombs, or one 500 lb bomb and six rockets, for flak suppression. A few carried the larger 11 inch 'Tiny Tim' rockets. The Panthers would be launched in three flights, the first fifty minutes after the strike group, the second and third at fifteen-minute intervals afterwards. The first flight of jets would catch up the strike group and accompany it in, the second flight would give air cover while the strike was in progress, and the third would cover the strike group as it retired.

Task Force 77 was steaming off the east coast, and the carrier aircraft therefore had to fly 225 miles overland across a mountain range, often in poor visibility and heavy overcast, to find and attack their main targets which were the bridges at Sinuiju on the west coast. They flew strikes on eight days between 9 and 21 November, making 593 sorties against the bridges, dropping 232 tons of bombs. For such an intense flying effort, the results were not outstanding: one highway bridge at Sinuiju destroyed for certain, and two at Hyesanjin, further inland, of which one was shared with a B–29 Superfortress.

As they went in to make their strikes, the carrier pilots could look over the Yalu river and see enemy MiG–15s taking off from the airfield at Amtung, on the Manchurian border. Enemy air activity was increasing ominously. Six Mig–15s appeared over Namsidong on 1 November and attacked four USAF P.51 Mustangs. On the 8th, a B–29 tail-gunner was credited with shooting down the first MiG.

It was clear from the start that the MiG–15s had a better rate of climb, greater speed, shorter turning radius and better manoeuvrabilty than the Panthers. The Navy pilots had to rely on better team-work and greater accuracy. A Panther pilot from *Philippine Sea* shot down a MiG on the 9th, and one Panther from *Leyte* and two from *Valley Forge* shot down two more MiGs on the 18th. No Navy aircraft were lost or damaged.

By the end of November, bombing of the Yalu bridges became irrelevant. The river was freezing over and the communists could cross virtually where they pleased. On the 29th, the primary mission of the carriers reverted to close air support. It was not before time. Suddenly, the war had taken a turn for the worse for the United Nations.

Retreat to Hungnam

By the end of October 1950, it seemed that the UN forces in Korea were on the brink of complete victory. Elements of Eighth Army in the west and X Corps in the east were both approaching the Yalu river. At sea, UN warships held both coasts in a tight blockade. UN aircraft ranged almost at will over the plains and mountains of Korea, choosing targets as they pleased up to the Manchurian border. In the battle there came a welcome lull which, however, made some less complacent members of UN staff uneasy.

On the morning of 24 November, Eighth Army began an offensive which was intended to push the North Korean Army back against the Yalu and end the war. But, at sunset on the 25th, the communists struck back with a powerful (and, by UN intelligence staff, completely unforeseen and unforecast) counter-stroke which rapidly expanded into a major offensive. Far from advancing, UN forces were forced to give ground, and in some cases to begin a full-scale retreat.

The main attack was in the northern central Korean mountains between Eighth Army and X Corps, forcing a gap through which poured tens of thousands of Red Chinese soldiers. In the east, X Corps was by then strung out all the way from Hungnam almost to

Retreat to Hungnam: smoke and flames of close air support to Marine units on the ground

31

Winter in Korea: Machinist's
Mate Harry S. Meredith working
on a Skyraider of USS
Philippine Sea, November 1950

the Manchurian border, a distance of some 100 miles. The 5th and 7th Regiments of the 1st Marine Division were holding Yudam-ni, near the Chosin reservoir. At 2200 on the night of 27 November, at least 60,000 and possibly as many as 100,000 Chinese troops hurled themselves against the Marines' defensive perimeter. The Chinese attacked first by squads and then, when those were wiped out, by companies, and finally in massed regiments, shouting and yelling and whistling and blowing horns as they advanced. By dawn, they had worked round behind Yudam-ni and cut off the Marines from the south.

On the morning of the 28th, Marine Corsairs from *Sicily* and *Badoeng Strait* flew over Yudam-ni, expecting to cover a Marine advance towards Kangye. But, briefed by radio, they turned instead to searching the countryside around for Chinese formations gathering to attack. At noon on the 30th, some 2,000 Chinese were reported north of the Marines' position. Marine Corsairs at once began to bomb and strafe the area, reducing the Chinese strength by about a half. When, at about 3 pm, the Chinese ran down the hillside to attack with their usual orchestration of shouts, whistles and bugle calls, four Marine Corsairs overhead, loaded with napalm, peeled off at 5,000 feet and screamed down to make their bombing runs 'on the deck'. As the fourth Corsair released its napalm, the first was back to strafe the Chinese with cannon shells. The attack lost its momentum and the surviving Chinese retreated over the nearest crest. Elsewhere around Yudam-ni Corsairs and Skyraiders from *Philippine Sea* and *Leyte* also bombed and strafed Chinese positions.

On 2 December, the Marines broke out from Yudam-ni to retreat first the fifteen miles to Hagaru-ri and eventually to the sea at Hungnam, sixty miles away. They took with them their wounded and their equipment; only the dead were left behind, buried with full military honours.

The 'Hungnam Redeployment', as it was called, was one of the great fighting performances of the US Marine Corps. It was a retreat through a mountainous, hostile countryside, swarming with Chinese snipers. Night-time temperatures fell well below freezing. A bitter wind blew constantly from the north. There was a foot of snow on the road, and every mile was obstructed by roadblocks. There were booby traps and mines.

The Marines were supported every step of the way by aircraft from *Sicily* and *Badoeng Strait* and from Task Force 77. Above the long column of marching men the aircraft circled, always ready to be called down by the Marines' controllers to clear roadblocks or to disperse Chinese with bombs, rockets and cannon shells. Sometimes the aircraft dropped their napalm so close ahead the Marines could actually feel the heat of it on their cheeks. 'Occasionally we caught the white-uniformed Chinese troops in the open,' said Commander Horace H. Epes, commanding *Leyte*'s Corsair squadron, VF–33. 'I vividly recall catching a couple of Red

US Navy F4U Corsair firing an anti-tank 'Ram' rocket over Korea, October 1950. Inset: A bridge in North Korea after an attack by Fireflies from HMS *Theseus*

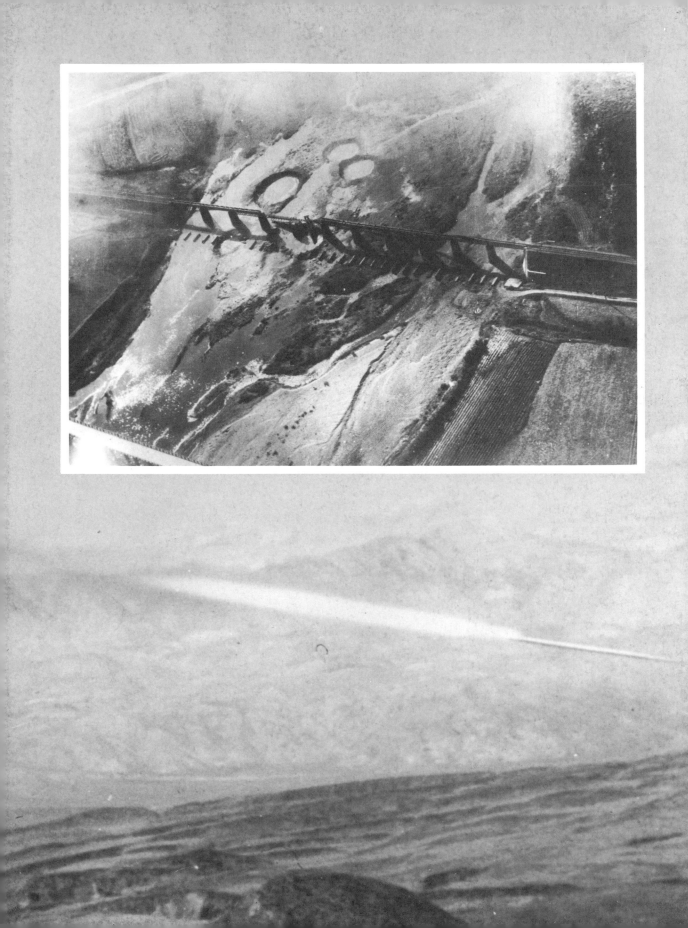

soldiers hotfooting it down the road carrying a long pole with a big kettle of what looked like soup – that no one ever drank.'

On 4 December, the commanding general of the First Marine Aircraft Wing signalled Commander Task Force 77 (Rear Admiral Edward C. Ewen): 'I was up on the hill today (at Hagaru-ri) and saw the Fifth and Seventh Marines return. They thanked God for air. I don't think they could have made it as units without air support. The next job is to get them off this hill. I want to be able to cover their flanks and rear one hundred per cent, and to blast any major resistance to their front. Can use all the help you can give me until they get down. Tell your pilots they are doing a magnificent job.'

That day the aircraft responded by flying 239 close support sorties controlled by the Marine tactical controller: 128 by TF 77, 34 by the CVEs *Sicily* and *Badoeng Strait*, and another 77 by Marine aircraft flying from their base at Yompo.

Inevitably the Marines incurred casualties, but aircraft took them to safety. The Marines bulldozed short airstrips out of the frozen and rocky ground at Hagaru-ri and Koto-ri from which USAF C–47s and Marine R4Ds evacuated a total of 4,675 wounded and frostbite cases.

At Koto-ri on 8 December the Marines arrived at a deep gorge where the bridge had been blown. There were steep cliffs on either side, so no vehicles, artillery or tanks could bypass the road. Without a bridge, the Marines would have to abandon their heavy equipment. Eight USAF C–119 Flying Boxcars each flew in with a metal bridging span weighing two tons. Under fire, the Marines built a new bridge with the eight spans and crossed the ravine.

For the final evacuation from Hungnam, the Navy and Marines provided air cover from seven carriers: TF 77 now had *Philippine Sea*, *Valley Forge*, *Leyte* and *Princeton* (with CAG 19, of a Panther squadron, two Corsair squadrons and a Skyraider squadron), while *Sicily* and *Badoeng Strait* of TG 96.8 had been joined by *Bataan*. A curtain of steel was also laid down by gunfire from thirteen warships, including the battleship USS *Missouri*.

Each day, as ships left with troops on board, the Hungnam perimeter was allowed to contract. Carrier aircraft flew 1,700 sorties inside the perimeter and as many more deep into enemy-held territory, while the gunfire support ships fired 22,000 rounds, from 16 inch down to 40 mm, and 1,500 rockets. Every night the sky blazed with tracer and starshell. Engineers and demolition teams blew up anything of value on the shore side. In all, some 105,000 US and Korean military personnel and 91,000 civilian refugees were taken off, with 17,500 vehicles and 350,000 tons of cargo.

There were similar evacuations at Wonsan, and at Chinnampo on the west coast, where three Canadian, two Australian and one US destroyer carried out a very daring night passage up the river, negotiating a channel thirty miles long in darkness to take off evacuees. Air cover was provided by Sea Furies and Fireflies of HMS *Theseus*.

At 1436 on 24 December, *Philippine Sea* signalled that the evacuation was complete. The last pilot to fly over Hungnam, in a Corsair from *Princeton*, saw from his 'grandstand seat' at 15,000 feet 'the most dismal and distressing sight I ever witnessed. Haze was everywhere. The artificial haze of war – one part hate, one part frustration, stirred to an even pall by high explosives. There were fires everywhere through the area, and, as I watched, flames broke out around the docks, growing and spreading until the whole water front seemed ablaze. As I took departure for *Princeton*, I called for the *Mount McKinley* [the command ship] and we exchanged greetings. "Merry Christmas" we said, for it was Christmas Eve 1950 . . .'

The Light Brigade – HMS *Theseus*

While the American carriers operated almost exclusively on the east coast, a single British (and, later, an Australian) light fleet carrier worked the west coast. The experience of HMS *Theseus* from October 1950 until she was relieved by HMS *Glory* in April 1951, during which time she made eight patrols 'up the coast', illustrated the problems encountered by one carrier operating by herself.

Theseus normally patrolled in the Yellow Sea off the Shantung Peninsula of China. Her CAG 17 had twenty-three Sea Furies, twelve Fireflies and one Sea Otter or, latterly, a helicopter. Although the submarine risk was very slight, one Firefly, fitted with a 55-gallon long-range tank instead of radar, flew anti-submarine patrols. This patrol was often useful for investigating surface contacts. A CAP of Sea Furies was maintained throughout daylight hours. When the wind dropped away, RATOG (rocket assisted take-off gear) was used. *Theseus* had a single but efficient catapult. In the spring of 1951, when operating with USS *Bataan*, her one catapult could keep pace with the American carrier's two.

Theseus' aircraft were hard-worked, on a variety of tasks: armed reconnaissance, strikes against pre-briefed targets, and close support for the troops ashore, the sorties being controlled by the Joint Operational Centre, at Seoul, and then at Taegu; photo-reconnaissance; interdiction strikes against roads and railways; bombardment spotting, off Inchon in January 1951, and off Wonsan on the east coast in April in company with *Bataan*. No night operations were flown but aircraft regularly took off before dawn, to keep crews familiar with the flight deck drills and procedures in darkness.

None of *Theseus'* aircraft ever engaged in combat with the enemy, but they did intercept literally thousands of friendly aircraft, many of them USAF medium bombers. The CAPs were useful in spotting snowstorms, so that the ship could steer clear. It was important to keep the flight deck as clear of snow as possible. In the bitter and unremitting cold of a Korean winter, everything on the flight deck was frozen solid in the mornings. Flight deck personnel had to be properly clad, in clothing loose enough to allow them to work but warm enough for the long periods of standing about in the open during the frequent gales and snow squalls – despite which *Theseus* achieved seventeen flying days in December.

Aircraft, fitted with 45-gallon drop tanks, normally flew 2½-hour sorties. A normal flying day had five 2½-hour details, for an average of about fifty, up to a maximum of sixty-six, sorties a day. With a supply line of 12,000 miles back to the United Kingdom, great care had to be taken with aircraft and spares. Replacement aircraft were brought up from Singapore by the replenishment carrier HMS *Unicorn*, whose work in the Korean campaign was unobtrusive but vital, and flown off to the operational carriers as necessary. Time-expired or 'dud' aircraft were transferred to *Unicorn* and thence taken back to harbour. Good drill was essential to minimize damage and wastage. *Theseus* had only five barrier crashes in her operational tour and in three of those a late arrester wire was engaged and the damage was repairable on board. From 1 December 1950 to 1 February 1951 there was only one slight propeller 'peck' by a Firefly on landing, out of a total of 1,236 landings. (When CAG 17 left in May 1951 they had built up a sequence of 800 accident-free landings.)

Four of *Theseus*' pilots were rescued from behind enemy lines, and four were picked up from the sea by helicopter. For the last patrol an S–51 Sikorsky helicopter was embarked, which was fitted with an 'anti-coning' device which allowed it to operate from the flight deck in wind speeds up to 35–40 knots (instead of only about 22 knots).

In six and a half months of operations, with a three-week break in Hong Kong, *Theseus*' aircraft flew 3,489 operational sorties. Six officers were promoted from the ship, and CAG 17 won the 1951 Boyd Trophy, the Fleet Air Arm's premier award for outstanding service.

The Bridges at Toko-ri

In January 1951 the Army asked if Task Force 77 could undertake the cutting of railway lines, and attack key bridges and railway rolling stock. At first, Vice Admiral Arthur D. Struble, commanding the Seventh Fleet, demurred. He considered, quite rightly, that naval aircraft were better employed in close support, as they had been during the retreat to Hungnam. But, after carrying out a comprehensive photographic survey to identify the best targets, TF 77 began in February upon a task which was nothing less than an attempt to make the entire east coast Korean railway system unworkable.

One of the first bridges to be identified was just south of the important rail, road and river junction of Kilchu, in the north-east of Korea. It spanned what became known as 'Carlson's Canyon', so

HMS *Theseus* in Korea. Top: US
helicopter landing on the flight
deck, USS *Bataan* ahead.
Centre: Leaving Sasebo, Japan,
homeward bound, 25 April
1951. Bottom: Firefly of 810
Squadron bombing the dock
area at Chinnampo

called after Lieutenant Commander Harold G. ('Swede') Carlson, commanding *Princeton*'s Skyraider squadron, VA–195, who devoted a great deal of attention and bombing to it. Supposed to be the original of the bridge at Toko-ri in James Michener's novel, the bridge was 600 feet long, and had five concrete piers supporting six steel spans. There were two railway tunnels at each end. It was a perfect target.

The bridge was first attacked on 2 March, with only minor damage to the approaches. On the 3rd, Carlson and his Skyraiders dropped one span, and damaged a second. On the 7th, another span was dropped. But by the 14th it was seen that the bridge was well on the way to being repaired and would be serviceable again in a few days. On the 15th it was attacked with napalm, which burned the new wooden structures under the original spans. A third span was destroyed and a fourth badly damaged. Only two of the original spans still stood. But, two weeks later, the bridge had been almost completely repaired. In more raids on 2 April, all the spans were knocked down. Now, at last, the communists gave up and began to build a bypass on lower ground.

By the end of April 1951, air attacks had reduced rail traffic to half the normal. In some places, for much of the time, traffic had been cut to nothing. But the stoppages were only temporary. As the number of sorties flown, tons of bombs dropped, and bridges, locomotives and rolling stock destroyed mounted to astronomical figures, it was clear that air attack alone was not enough. Whenever the carriers were diverted, as they were to the Straits of Formosa at the beginning of April, or went back to close support, as when the enemy launched a fresh offensive on 22 April, the communists made giant strides in repairing the rail system.

They were indefatigable, swarming like worker ants over the bridges and formations at night or whenever overcast weather prevented flying. If the east coast system was temporarily out of action, then the communists simply put more traffic onto the west. They made more use of Korea's primitive roads, which were largely unmetalled and so rudimentary as not to make worthwhile targets for air attack. They used horses, and mules, and even camels. Above all, they walked, with soldiers and coolies carrying prodigious loads on bamboo frames on their backs.

The aircraft carriers returned to the interdiction campaign, as it was called, on 1 May. *Boxer*, which had relieved *Valley Forge* in March and had the first reserve carrier air group, CVG–101, embarked, *Princeton* and *Philippine Sea* destroyed thirty-one rail bridges and their bypasses and eleven road bridges and bypasses in thirteen days. But, as the battle ashore swayed to and fro, the carrier aircraft went from interdiction to close support and back to interdiction again. For the new communist offensive on 16 May, the UN counter-attack on the 21st, and until 1 June, the carriers were on close support, thus giving time for the railways to be repaired. On 2 June, the carriers resumed interdiction and in nine days completely destroyed twenty-four rail bridges and bypasses, and six road bridges and bypasses. In some of these attacks, on a bridge near the coast at Songjin, Panther jets took part in bombing raids for the first time. But twice more in July this bridge was destroyed and twice again it was repaired.

Very occasionally, a special target required special methods. In April the communists were using the dam at Hwachon to regulate the water level in the Pukhan and Han rivers, lowering the water to fordable level when they themselves were advancing, but flooding the area when the UN were advancing. On 30 April, six Skyraiders from *Princeton* (led by Carlson), escorted by Corsairs for flak-suppression, dive-bombed the dam but did not damage the sluicegates. Next day, eight Skyraiders made a second attack, this time with torpedoes set to run shallow. Six of the torpedoes ran true and hit. One sluicegate was destroyed, a second had a ten-foot hole blown in it, and the waters in the reservoir were released.

Operation Strangle

As General MacArthur said, with the entry of the Chinese it became a new war. MacArthur himself believed, and frequently proclaimed, that victory could only be won by extending the conflict beyond Korea 'against the nerve centre of the Chinese ability to sustain his operations in Korea' – by which he meant mainland China. Here, he clashed with the political judgement of President Truman and consequently suffered his famous dismissal on 11 April 1951. He was replaced by General Matthew Ridgway who had arrived in Korea after General Walker had been killed in a jeep accident on 23 December 1950. Ridgway had set about restoring the somewhat tattered morale of Eighth Army. He also brought it and X Corps under unified command. Ridgway now became C-in-C United Nations Command.

In February 1951, the United Nations had begun Operation KILLER, to inflict the maximum number of casualties upon the Chinese, rather than capture or recapture territory. But the UN planning staffs always cherished the dream of using their over-whelming carrier- and land-based air power to subjugate Korea, to cut the country into manageable sections, and inhibit the enemy's power to move and to fight by interdiction strikes against his communications and, later, his industrial base.

Thus, in June 1951, Operation STRANGLE began. An imaginary strip, one degree of latitude in width, from 38° 15'N to 39° 15'N, which was just behind the Chinese front line, was drawn across the country. The traffic networks across it were divided into eight routes. The Fifth Air Force in Korea was given the three westernmost routes. The First Marine Air Wing took the three easternmost, while TF 77 had the two centre routes. The air forces were to destroy every bridge, every vehicle, every target within their own sectors. Selected valleys and mountain passes were designated as 'strangle areas' or 'choke points', marked for special attention.

For several weeks aircraft bombed bridges, blew craters in roads and rail tracks, fired rockets into tunnels, strafed vehicles, sowed 'butterfly' anti-personnel bombs and delayed-action bombs fused to explode after 6–72 hours. On 20 June TF 77's aircraft dropped half a million leaflets. Searchlights, flares and 'night heckling' aircraft were used to prevent the enemy travelling after dark.

But it was like trying to subdue an ant hill with a fly swat. The communists, with seemingly inexhaustible reserves of labour and of fatalism, filled in the craters, relaid the tracks, rebuilt the bridges or, when all else failed, walked round. They blew up the butterfly bombs with rifle fire, or just ignored them. They worked on around delayed-action bombs, accepting the risks of being blown up.

In October, the carriers *Bon Homme Richard*, *Antietam* and *Essex* whose air group included a squadron of the new McDonnell F2H2 Banshee jet fighters, went back to track-busting and rail-cutting. Lines were cut in a thousand places. Hundreds of yards of track were torn up. But the enemy repaired them, ran shuttle services, and cannibalized points and other fittings, taking them to where they were most needed.

Pilots returning to Korea for their second tours remarked that enemy flak had intensified tenfold since their first visits. Flak had been present from the earliest days, but there was no doubt that it was steadily increasing in frequency and accuracy. The enemy were also very quick to notice shifts in target emphasis, moving their anti-aircraft batteries from bridges to track-sides and back again, as a pattern of attacks developed.

For the first time, carriers began to experience problems with aircrew morale. 'One of my toughest jobs,' said Commander M.U. Beebe, commanding *Essex*'s Air Group Five, 'was the constant battle to keep pilots' morale up. Day after day, for weeks on end, pilots had to fly over the same area of Korea, bombing bridges or punching holes in railbeds. The anti-aircraft fire over Korea grew steadily heavier, more accurate, and more intense. From 22 August until 30 November 1951, Air Group Five's aircraft were struck 318 times, resulting in 27 aircraft losses, and the loss of 11 pilots.

'A pilot would go out one day, do a first-rate bombing job on a bridge or leave several craters in a railbed, and come back the next day and find that all the damage had been repaired overnight. It was hard for him to see how his efforts were having any effect on the course of the fighting. Any pilot could scour an undefended section of the countryside, avoiding the flak areas. But in places like "Death Valley", west of Wonsan, it required a skilful and courageous pilot to weave his way through a maze of well-defended antiaircraft positions and still get a hit. This type of war was a new challenge.'

Bombing run by Skyraider on a bridge in North Korea, October 1951

West Coast Story

Operation STRANGLE had been a failure. Although the UN Command had to make their decisions within a strict political straitjacket, they might have gained from a more fluid approach to the war, instead of the somewhat static campaign they actually fought. As General James van Fleet, Commander of Eighth Army, commented later, 'We fought the Communist on his own terms, even though we had the advantages of flexibility, mobility, and firepower. We fought *his* way, which was terrible. We both sat, and dug in, and he was the superior rat. He was small; he could dig holes faster; and if he lost a hundred people in a hole, he'd just go out and find another hundred.'

Nevertheless, by June 1951, in van Fleet's opinion, 'we had the Chinese whipped. They were definitely gone. They were in awful shape. During the last week of May we captured more than 10,000 prisoners. It was a short time later that the Reds asked for a truce.'

The truce talks begun that summer lasted, with breaks, for two years, and even then produced only an armistice (which is still in force at the time of writing). Meanwhile, the situation on land stabilized around the 38th Parallel. At sea, the watch on both coasts was kept up, with Task Force 95, which included ships of the Royal, Canadian, Australian, New Zealand, Netherlands, Siamese, South Korean and US Navies, working on the west coast as hard, for even less visible reward and much less media attention, than those on the east.

Above: Hawker Sea Fury FBII taking a wire on HMS *Glory*

Opposite above: McDonnell F2H Banshee from USS *Essex*. The Banshee, first twin-jet fighter to see action in Korea, made its first strike against the enemy on 21 August 1951

Below: USS *Antietam* operating with Task Force 77 off the east coast of Korea, October 1951

45

After relieving *Theseus*, HMS *Glory* began the first of her three tours of duty off the Korean coast on 3 May, operating with *Bataan*. Her CAG 14 had twenty-one Sea Fury XIs of 804 Squadron, and twelve Firefly Vs of 812 Squadron. For them the weather in the Yellow Sea in May and June was often foggy and drizzly. But in fine weather, they operated a fourteen-hour flying day, with some fifty to sixty sorties. *Glory* normally worked a nine-day operational cycle, flying for four days, replenishing for one day, returning for a second four-day period and then handing over to *Bataan*, returning to Kure or Sasebo in Japan for maintenance, and then sailing for another nine-day cycle.

By 22 June, *Glory*'s air group had expended some 60,000 rounds of 20 mm ammunition, over 1,000 rockets and 180 bombs whilst

racking up a tremendous tally of junks, bridges, buildings, stores, gun batteries and 109 ox carts (part of an ammunition train) destroyed. On 24 June, the first anniversary of the war, *Glory*'s aircraft attacked along almost the whole Korean front, the Fireflies bombing a railway bridge at Hwasanni and the Sea Furies giving close support to the troops.

Like the Americans, *Glory*'s aircrew found that enemy flak was gaining in quantity and accuracy, with a marked increase in small arms fire. The enemy were making more use of flak traps and camouflaged dummies, and were holding their fire until aircraft had completed their dives and were pulling away. *Glory*'s pilots soon learned not to dally at low level, but to make one attack only, with aircraft attacking from different angles. Even so, more than

Firefly, armed with two 500 lb bombs, preparing to take off from HMAS *Sydney*

half of *Glory*'s thirty-three aircraft were hit by flak on her last patrol. Two Sea Furies and two Fireflies were lost to enemy action. All but the pilot of one of the Fireflies were recovered. *Glory* started her last patrol on 21 September, when she raised the light fleet carrier record for daily sorties to eighty-four, and then left for refit in Australia.

Glory's relief was HMAS *Sydney*, the first Dominion aircraft carrier ever to go into action, with Sea Furies of 805 and 808 Squadrons and Fireflies of 817. *Sydney* began on the west coast on 4 October but soon went round to the east to operate for a time. On 11 October, she broke the light fleet record with 89 sorties in a day and 147 over two days. But *Glory* returned in January 1952 and put the record up to 104 sorties.

Another light fleet carrier, HMS *Ocean*, arrived in May 1952. She and *Glory* operated in turn off the west coast, and also with USS *Badoeng Strait* and *Bairoko*, until the armistice in July 1953 and for a time afterwards. *Ocean* had a very keen air group, of 802 Squadron Sea Furies and 825 Squadron Fireflies, who achieved landing intervals of 18.6 seconds for four Sea Furies and 20.2 seconds for Fireflies. They also put the daily light fleet record up to 123, and won the Boyd Trophy for 1952.

Ocean was the only carrier to experience serious enemy air opposition off the west coast. On 27 July 1952, four Fireflies were attacked by two MiG–15s. Two Fireflies were damaged. One landed safely on board, the other ashore. Shortly afterwards, four Sea Furies were attacked by four MiGs but it was a very brief encounter and no damage was done.

On 9 August, four Sea Furies were attacked by eight MiGs at 5,000 feet. It was a brief dogfight in which one MiG was shot down. 'My No. 2, Sub-Lt. Carl Haines, said "MiGs five o'clock",' recalled the flight leader, Lieutenant P. ('Hoagy') Carmichael. 'I did not see them at first, and my No. 4 Sub-Lt. Smoo Ellis gave a break. We all turned towards the MiGs. Two went for my Nos 3 and 4 Lt. Pete Davies and Sub-Lt. Ellis. They were seen to get good hits on one who broke away with smoke coming from him.'

Later the same day, four Sea Furies were jumped by four MiGs at 6,000 feet. One MiG was seen to break away trailing a cloud of black smoke. One Sea Fury had a drop tank set on fire but succeeded in extinguishing it by side-slipping and returned on board. An hour later two Sea Furies met two MiGs at 4,000 feet and one Sea Fury had to make a forced landing on an island. Next day, four Sea Furies were engaged by another eight MiGs. One MiG left the scene smoking but was not actually seen to crash. 'The impression we got was that the first MiG pilots were very inexperienced,' said Carmichael, 'but the next day we had an engagement with eight MiGs and we were very lucky to get away with it. I reckon they must have sent their instructors down!' The final score was one MiG, two probables and two damaged, against two Sea Furies damaged.

'Moonlight Sonata' and 'Insomnia'

With hindsight it can be seen that, by January 1952, land- and carrier-based air power, no matter how many aircraft were used nor how bravely and skilfully they were flown, was not enough. Decisive movement on the ground, coupled with some political developments, were also needed to bring the war to a conclusion.

Nevertheless, the TF 77 carriers on the east coast opened the new year with fresh plans, particularly for night operations, using specially equipped night versions of the Corsair, the F4U5N, and the Skyraider, the AD4N.

They began on 15 January with Operation MOONLIGHT SONATA, a 'night heckling' operation against railways, designed to take advantage of the winter snow and bright moonlight, when roads, rails, hills and valleys would be easy to see at night from the air.

At 3 am every morning, ten aircraft were launched, in pairs, each section of two being given a fifty-mile stretch of railway and briefed on the best targets. The snow was abundant enough, but bright moonlight, good flying weather and suitable targets rarely coincided. Some locomotives were found but in general the results were disappointing. Furthermore, trains began to appear just as the aircraft were leaving. Unsurprisingly, the communists had worked out the timetable. So, Operation INSOMNIA was launched, with aircraft being flown off an hour earlier. But this too was discontinued in mid March.

In the first six months of 1952, an enormous effort was devoted to 'track-busting', using napalm, bombs and, later, the 2.75 inch folding-fin 'Mighty Mouse' rocket. In February, 1,037 breaks were made in railway lines. In April, May and June, over 7,000 sorties were flown, to achieve another 3,000 cuts, with 80 bridges and 100 bypasses destroyed. In the twenty months since carrier aircraft first began to try and strangle the enemy supply lines, more than 13,000 breaks had been made in rail tracks, and 500 bridges and 300 bridge bypasses had been destroyed in north-eastern Korea.

Once again, the overall results did not justify the effort. The enemy's supply lines were certainly not strangled. Furthermore, there was always a tendency for the air war in Korea to become fixed in certain patterns. Aircraft tended to appear at certain times. Night attacks arrived just after sunset, or three hours before dawn. The sight of coloured smoke flares, or coloured front-line panels being laid out, warned the enemy in the trenches opposite to expect close support missions. Thus the enemy, who was by no means unintelligent, could very often make a shrewd guess at the time and even the direction aircraft would approach.

In June 1952, the carriers switched to industrial targets, with much less emphasis on interdiction. For the carrier air groups, this was a very welcome change. The US Navy had four carriers, normally operating two off the coast at a time but occasionally carrying out major operations to coincide with change-over periods so that all·four carriers could take part.

On 23 June, *Boxer* and *Princeton* were joined by *Bon Homme Richard* and *Philippine Sea* for a four-day series of strikes by Navy, Marine and Fifth Air Force aircraft on thirteen power plants in North Korea, including the fourth largest hydro-electric plant in the world, at Suiho, on the Yalu river, which supplied both North Korea and Manchuria. Until then Suiho had been spared from attack because, first, it was thought the war would soon be over and the repair bill would have to be met by the American taxpayer, then, after Inchon, so as not to give the Chinese a pretext to enter the war and, finally, so as not to prejudice the progress of the armistice talks. After two years of war and one year of talks, the time for such sensibilities was long past.

At 2 pm on the 23rd, the carriers began to fly off the first of thirty-five Skyraiders, thirty-one of them carrying two 2,000 lb bombs and one 1,000 lb bomb each, while four Skyraiders had survival packs, to drop to anyone shot down, in lieu of the 1,000 lb bomb. As the Skyraiders crossed the coastline, they were overhauled by thirty-five Panther jets which had taken off fifty minutes later. The weather was perfect: cloudy on the approach, clearing over the target. In 'MiG Alley', along the Yalu, the strike force met eighty-four F86 Sabre jets of the Fifth Air Force already orbiting over the target. Numerous MiGs were spotted on the airfield at Amtung, but although some took off, they flew to the north and, for some unexplained reason, none took any part in the action.

As the flak-suppression Panthers strafed the guns along the river, the Skyraiders 'pushed over' into their dives at 5,000 feet released bombs at 3,000 and pulled out at 1,500. All went well and in less than two minutes the Skyraiders had dropped nearly 90 tons of bombs, and escaped almost unscathed. Five Skyraiders were hit by flak, and one had to make a wheels-up landing at Kimpo.

While the Skyraiders were withdrawing, seventy-nine F84 Thunderjets and forty-nine F80 Shooting Stars of Fifth Air Force dropped 145 tons of bombs in a co-ordinated strike. Meanwhile, seventy-five Marine aircraft bombed Chosin power plant. A second TF 77 strike of ninety aircraft and fifty-two USAF aircraft struck at Fusen. A third carrier strike of that day, with seventy aircraft, hit Kyosen. The following day, TF 77, Marine and USAF aircraft struck at Suiho, Fusen and Kyosen again. TF 77 aircraft flew 546 sorties over the thirteen power plants on the 23rd and 24th. The USAF returned to Chosin and Fusen on the 26th and 27th. About ninety per cent of North Korean power production was disabled and almost the whole country was blacked out for a fortnight. Power supplies had not returned to normal by the end of the year.

After such a success, an even bigger coup was planned, against the North Korean capital of Pyongyang itself. The city was a notorious 'flak trap', ringed by at least fifty heavy and more than a hundred light AA guns. There were POW camps on its outskirts.

The first guided missiles. Opposite above: A 'drone' pilotless radio-controlled F6F Hellcat being launched from USS *Boxer*, 1 September 1952, and (below) being joined by its controlling 'mother plane'. Left: The 'drone' exploding on its target, a railway tunnel in North Korea, while the 'mother' turns away to return (below) to the *Boxer*

Lt-Cdr W.C. Maurer operates the 'drone' by remote control during trials on board USS *Shangri-La*

On 11 July, forty-five aircraft from *Bon Homme Richard* and forty-six from *Princeton* attacked targets in the south-eastern part of the city. While F86 Sabres established a barrier patrol over 'MiG Alley' to prevent interference, aircraft from Fifth Air Force, the Marines, the Royal Australian Air Force and from HMS *Ocean* attacked targets assigned to them all over the city, the idea being that these air groups would relieve each other and thus keep up the attacks all day, giving the defences no respite.

Although the flak was the heaviest some pilots had ever seen ('It was so thick,' one said, 'we could have dropped our wheels and landed on the stuff') a total of 1,400 tons of bombs and 23,000 gallons of napalm were delivered by 1,254 aircraft. Pyongyang radio was off the air for two days and when it resumed it stated that 1,500 buildings had been destroyed and 900 damaged in the raid.

The attacks became ever bigger and bolder. A second raid, of 1,403 sorties, was made on Pyongyang on 29 August. On twelve days of July 1952, TF 77 aircraft attacked a range of industrial targets, including the Sindok lead and zinc mill on 27 July and the Kilchu magnesite plant on the 28th. On 1 September the largest all-Navy air strike of the war, twenty-nine aircraft from *Essex*, sixty-three from *Princeton*, and fifty-two from *Boxer*, destroyed the Aoji oil refinery, in the top north-eastern corner of Korea. For variety, Guided missile Unit 90, embarked in *Boxer*, launched six attacks on selected bridges with 'Drones': pilotless radio-controlled ex-Second World War F6F Hellcats, loaded with explosive and fitted with a TV guidance system, which were conducted to their targets by control aircraft. This was a very early use of guided missiles from carriers.

With seemingly unlimited supplies of aircraft, and a new concept, of a carrier air task group commander to improve the control over large numbers of aircraft taking part in a strike, TF 77 was becoming capable of launching ever bigger and more devastating strikes. But, ironically, the diminishing demand for interdiction and the dwindling number of industrial objectives meant that, by October 1952, TF 77 was running out of targets.

'Cherokee'

In May 1952, Rear Admiral J.J. 'Jocko' Clark, who had commanded TF 77 briefly in 1951, was promoted Vice Admiral in command of Seventh Fleet. 'Jocko' was an experienced carrier admiral, having commanded a task group in the Pacific under Spruance and Halsey. Flying over Korea, 'Jocko' noticed beneath him dozens of UN supply depots, vehicle parks, personnel housing and ammunition dumps. He reasoned that the enemy, though an expert at camouflage and an indefatigable tunneller, would also have such targets out in the open. TF 77 was therefore set to attack these targets in what were called 'Cherokee' strikes ('Jocko' was a full-blooded Cherokee Indian).

They began in mid-October 1952 and, after some initial mis-understandings over control, got properly under way in November. Again, they made a pleasant change of targets for TF 77 aircrews, who raked over the autumn countryside with napalm and 2,000 lb bombs, the only ones which could collapse the enemy's deep bunkers and tunnels. They were very effective; communist soldiers were frequently found entombed, their brains oozing from their ears. Occasionally, 'Cherokees' went in on friendly territory, causing casualties and adverse comment back home in the US.

For maximum effect, 'Cherokees' should have been co-ordinated with ground attacks but, while the armistice talks still continued, there was a virtual stalemate on all fronts. However, the 'Cherokees', which continued until the armistice in July 1953, were good for UN morale and highly approved by the Army. The ordinary soldier, in his boots, in the line, knew little and cared less about the niceties of the proper use of air power. What he wanted to see were lots of friendly aircraft clobbering the enemy on that opposite hillside with lots of bombs.

'Bedcheck Charlies'

Korea was a curious war for naval fighter pilots. They knew, mostly at second-hand, of the hectic air-to-air fighting in 'MiG Alley' where the USAF F86 Sabrejets used to rise high over North Korea, flying at 38,000–40,000 feet towards the Yalu river, the sun glinting on their silver wings and flashing on their cockpit domes, and the contrails streaming out behind them, like the plumes from a knight's helmet. Looking down to the north, they could see their opponents taking off from Amtung and Tatungkou. In dogfights, MiG and Sabre made head-on passes at combined speeds of more than 1,200 mph. Coming out of combat dives, pilots were subjected to gravity pulls of as much as 8G. The MiG was generally more effective at high altitudes, the Sabre at lower, but by good teamwork and accurate shooting the Sabres undoubtedly achieved the mastery; by July 1953, 802 MiGs had been shot down, to 56 Sabrejets – a ratio of nearly 14 to 1 in favour of the Sabrejets.

At sea, such chances of air-to-air combat were very rare. Only ten enemy aircraft were shot down by Navy and Marine pilots flying from carriers (although another forty-one were shot down by pilots flying with Fifth Air Force). The best day was 18 November 1952, when USS *Oriskany*, *Essex* and *Kearsarge* were operating in the north, only ninety miles south of Vladivostok. A CAP of four Panthers from *Kearsarge* encountered seven silver MiGs, believed to be Russian. The Panther section leader was restricted to 13,000 feet because of a fuel boost pump defect, but the other three pilots fought an eight-minute engagement in which they shot down two MiGs – one MiG, as the *Kearsarge* pilot who followed him down said, 'going into a deep graveyard spiral'.

The Navy's only 'ace', and only 'night ace', was Lieutenant Guy

B. Bordelon of *Princeton*. Towards the end of the war, the communists began to make night raids in the Inchon–Seoul–Kimpo area, using antique aircraft such as YAK 18s and aged Po.2 biplanes. These, known as 'Bedcheck Charlies', were much too slow for the modern F94 jets of Fifth Air Force or the Marines' F3D Skyknights to intercept. In June 1953, 'Jocko' Clark asked for the services of a Navy F4U Corsair squadron.

The Corsairs flew ashore, like hired gunslingers coming into town, and after a week's familiarization with Fifth Air Force, went into action. Bordelon shot down two YAK 18s and three PO.2s between 30 June and 16 July 1953. A night-fighter detachment of three Firefly Vs of 810 Squadron flew ashore from HMS *Ocean* in July and made thirty-one 'Bedcheck' sorties before turning to police duties, patrolling the demarcation line, after the armistice.

The End in Korea

The war ended in a final flurry, with two major communist offensives in June and July 1953. These may well have been largely motivated by 'face', and a desire to be seen to be on the offensive as the armistice talks at Panmunjon appeared to be reaching a conclusion. But TF 77 responded with the most intensive flying effort of the war by the four carriers *Philippine Sea*, *Boxer*, *Princeton*, and *Lake Champlain*. Total sorties rose from 4,343 in May 1953 to 6,423 in July; close support sorties rose from 256 to 1,690; and tons of bombs, rockets and cannon shells expended rose from 2,835 in May to 4,606 in July. The record for a day's sorties, 554, set on 13 June, was easily surpassed. The carriers flew 598 sorties on 24 July, 608 on the 25th and 649 on the 26th. On 23 July *Boxer* achieved her 61,000th deck landing, a fleet record.

The armistice was signed at 10 am on the morning of 27 July 1953, to come into effect at 10 pm that evening. For the carriers, that last day was like so many before it: the three carriers on station, *Philippine Sea*, *Boxer* and *Lake Champlain*, flew 250 sorties before 10 am, for 23 rail cars, 11 rail bridges, 1 tunnel, 69 buildings, 100 yards of trench and 9 road bridges destroyed or damaged. Forty rail and three road cuts were made.

The Korean war never excited much interest in the United Kingdom. Politicians persistently referred to it in the language of peacetime, as though it were a very minor 'bush-fire' affair. But in Korea the United States suffered casualties of 142,091 killed, wounded, missing or POW. The other UN contingents suffered total casualties of 17,260; the United Kingdom casualties were 686 dead, 2,498 wounded, 1,102 missing or POW – a total of 4,286. South Korean casualties were 1,313,836, including about a million civilians. Chinese casualties were estimated at about 900,000 men, the North Koreans 520,000 men and about one million civilians. Thus this little limited war at the other end of the world inflicted nearly four million casualties.

The Rise and Rise of the Helicopter

Helicopters landing troops to hunt Communists in Malaya

EVERY pilot who flew over Korea commented on the intensity of the flak, especially in the latter days. Five US Navy or Marine aircraft were lost in aerial combat in the Korean war – but a staggering total of 559 aircraft were shot down by anti-aircraft fire.

Most of the pilots survived, largely due to the work of the helicopters. There was something that greatly appealed to the imagination of the public in the images which emerged from the Korean war of the helicopters – 'handy andies', 'flying egg-beaters', 'gyrating angels', as they were variously called – thrashing and whirling down the valleys and across the paddy fields to pick up downed aircrew, whilst fixed-wing aircraft frequently flew CAPs overhead.

Every pilot whose aircraft was hit by flak tried to reach the sea if possible. The water was cold – in winter so very cold that a man had to be recovered within minutes before he froze to death – but it was still better than a North Korean POW camp. At sea, there was a very good chance of being picked up by the search and rescue helicopters who could recover aircrew from the water in a fifth of the time taken by even the most alert and well-trained seaguard destroyer – besides releasing that destroyer and her numerous crew for other duties. Early in the war, one of *Boxer*'s Corsairs suffered an engine failure on take-off and crashed into the sea in front of the ship. The helicopter had the pilot back on deck within three minutes, and this became a standard helicopter performance.

Later, LST 799 was converted into a helicopter base and landing ship – the first in naval history. On station off Wonsan harbour, she rescued twenty-four pilots – US Navy and Marines, British, and one South African – two by boat and the rest by her helicopters.

Helicopters were one of the main means of evacuating casualties: a wounded man could be picked up in the front line, a blood transfusion could be started before the helicopter left the ground and completed by the time the helicopter reached the Mobile Army Surgical Hospital. Of every 1,000 wounded men who reached hospital alive in the Second World War, 45 died; in Korea, only 25 out of every 1,000 were lost.

In Korea, the helicopter showed itself endlessly versatile. Demands arose from all sides and all ships to have helicopter platforms fitted. Helicopters acted as aerial staff cars; lifted patrols to command ground far ahead; took hot food to isolated outposts; carried mail or blood plasma to units in the line; located mines; flew protective reconnaissance on the flanks of an advancing force; chased and pinned down locomotives with gunfire; carried out spotting for bombarding ships; buoyed a crashed MiG in a river estuary, and then guided recovery vessels to the spot.

The main workhorse of the early days in Korea was a Sikorsky helicopter, S–51 in civilian life, known to the USAF as the H–5, to the US Navy as the HO3S, and to the Royal Navy as the Dragonfly HR–3. In the latter days, the S–51 was replaced by the larger S–55

(the H–19 Chickasaw, the Royal Navy's Westland Whirlwind). In one operation, twelve S–55s carried an entire battalion of 1,000 US Marines and their equipment sixteen miles over rugged country in four hours.

In February 1953, nine Dragonflies of 705 Squadron of the Fleet Air Arm took part in the biggest search and rescue operation up to that time, when they rescued more than 800 people from flooding in Holland (sixty-four people were actually winched up from their house-tops). In 1954, when there was widespread flooding in Pakistan, USAF H–5s were loaded onto C–124 Globemaster transport planes and flown direct from Korea to the disaster area.

In the Royal Navy, S–55s saw their first prolonged action during the Emergency in Malaya, where communist guerrillas and terrorists had been trying to seize control of the country since 1948. 848 Squadron, re-formed specifically for the task, were transported with their twelve American S–55s out to the Far East in 1953 in the repair carrier HMS *Perseus*.

Troops had sometimes been taking days to reach places in the jungle. With helicopters they could be lifted there in minutes. Helicopters could fly to positions which were no more than map references and land ten men at a time in jungle clearings surrounded by trees more than a hundred feet high. In Malaya, helicopters evacuated wounded, took tracker dogs to round up bandits and POWs back to base at Sembawang for interrogation, and dropped hundreds of tons of supplies – everything from ammunition to tractors. 848 Squadron were awarded the Boyd Trophy for 1954 and, in 1956, received an inscribed silver *kris*, the curved dagger which is the Malay national symbol, from a grateful government.

All Done by Mirrors
and Angles

Trials on the angled deck on
board USS *Antietam* in the
English Channel, July 1953

THERE were two ways of looking at the Korean war. Politically, it was claimed as a victory. An aggressor had been contained. A limited war had been fought to a limited conclusion, and had not escalated into a superpower confrontation. But militarily, it could be argued that Korea was a defeat. The means of defeating an enemy, though available, had not been used to defeat him. It was an invitation to a future aggressor.

However, Korea did show that there was no simple 'big bang' theory of national defence. Defence had a myriad facets, needed a whole range of graduated responses, was an infinitely complex problem, with no cheap single solution.

The victory, if it was a victory, in Korea was made possible by sea power, which had never been seriously disputed by the North Koreans or the Soviets. The great majority of the men and the great bulk of supplies had come by sea. Sea power had conferred upon the United Nations forces tremendous flexibility. The carriers of TF 77 and TF 95 had been able to exert their influence swiftly, either in the north or south, and on either coast.

Korea thus had a galvanizing effect upon naval air. Clearly, a new generation of aircraft and new aircraft carriers to operate them were at hand. The new aircraft would be bigger, faster and heavier. Therefore, the carriers must have larger hangars, longer and stronger flight decks, and reinforced lifts. Off Korea, every jet sortie had cost the host carrier an extra minute alongside a tanker, and every three-ton bomb load which left the deck meant another three minutes' replenishment alongside the ammunition ship. Therefore, carriers would require greater fuel and ammunition storage capacities. More aircraft would be operated. Therefore, the carriers would need newer, longer-range, more efficient radar, so as to be able to handle more aerial contacts simultaneously.

In the USA, Project 27A had begun in June 1948, to modernize the wartime *Essex* class carriers so that they could operate jets up to 40,000 lbs weight. The first was *Oriskany*, which then went to Korea, giving fresh impetus to the whole programme so that eventually ten more were similarly modernized. In July 1951, two years after the cancellation of the *United States*, a contract was awarded for the first of six *Forrestal* class, with an overall length of 1,000 feet, a displacement of 59,000 tons, which was almost twice that of the *Essex* class, and a speed of 33 knots. *Forrestal* herself was laid down on 14 July 1952. She was followed by *Saratoga* and *Ranger*, two famous US Navy carrier names.

In the United Kingdom, the 1952 Naval Estimates announced that existing carriers would be modernized, five new carriers were to be authorized, and 'many new aircraft of all types for the air force and the Navy' were promised. Of the wartime carriers, *Formidable* was reduced to reserve in 1948. *Victorious* was under reconstruction. *Illustrious* herself became training and trials carrier, and was then laid up in 1954. *Indomitable* was placed in reserve in 1954. So too were *Implacable* and *Indefatigable*. Of the light fleet carriers, many had been sold to foreign navies. But four of the 22,000 ton *Centaur* class were planned or already building. *Eagle* had commissioned, although the next *Ark Royal* was still some way in the future.

As the Korean war ended, the Douglas F4D Skyray, a supersonic fighter with a speed of about 750 mph, was just starting its sea trials with the fleet. The A3D Skywarrior, a twin-jet heavy attack aircraft, initially developed as a nuclear bomber but with a top speed equivalent to the 600 mph Banshee fighter, was already in production. The A4D Skyhawk, one of the most famous aircraft of the twentieth century, was building, and contracts had been let for the Chance Vought F8U–2 Crusader, an advanced fighter capable of speeds over 1,000 mph.

In the Royal Navy, the jet Attacker and the piston-engine Sea Fury were both replaced in 1953 by the Hawker Sea Hawk jet fighter, with a maximum speed of 560 mph. The twin piston-engine de Havilland Sea Hornet long-range fighter was succeeded in 1954 by the de Havilland Sea Venom, the Royal Navy's first all-weather jet fighter, with a maximum speed of 575 mph. For anti-submarine warfare, the Fairey Gannet entered front-line service in January 1955. The Royal Navy's strike aircraft of the 1950s was the 380 mph Westland Wyvern.

The much higher landing speeds and the rapidly increasing aircraft weights (for example, a wartime Seafire was 7,000 lbs, but by 1953 a fully-loaded Wyvern was 24,000 lbs) made obsolescent – and dangerous – the traditional method of working a flight deck, with arrester wires and crash barriers and the forward half in use as a deck park. Already, by 1953, 13,000 lb aircraft landing at 95 knots pulled out arrester wires so far that only one-third of the flight deck was available as a deck park, and there were even heavier and faster aircraft coming into service.

The solution, devised by Commander D.R.F. Cambell and Mr L. Boddington of the Royal Aircraft Establishment, Farnborough, was so staggeringly simple everybody else kicked themselves for not thinking of it. It was to slew the direction of the approach and landing a little out to port, so that if an aircraft missed the wires it could simply take off and go round again.

The first experiments, in HMS *Triumph* in 1952, were made by painting new lines on the flight deck, as were the trials on the 'axial deck', as it was first called in the US Navy, held in *Midway* in May 1952. Further trials required an extension of the flight deck out to port and realignment of the arrester wires. The first true angled deck (as it was ultimately called) was fitted for trials in USS *Antietam*. Between December 1952 and July 1953, 4,107 launches and landings were made, with no accident or incident of any kind which could be blamed on the angled deck. *Antietam* came to the United Kingdom in 1953, and British pilots were thus able to try out a British invention – on board an American ship. American carrier modernization plans were then modified, to include Project 27C – the incorporation of the angled deck.

HMS *Bulwark* with angled deck,
November 1954

The traditional Deck Landing Control Officer, or 'batsman', whose gestures and 'bats' indicated to an incoming pilot the correctness, or otherwise, of his landing approach, was also beginning to look old-fashioned. As landing speeds rose, while human reaction times remained the same, the time in which pilot and batsman could establish a rapport grew ever shorter. Some means was required whereby the pilot himself could monitor his own approach.

The mirror landing aid, originally devised by Commander H.C.N. Goodhart RN, consisted basically of a number of white lights shining into the curved inner surface of a concave mirror. The pilot flew so as to keep this apparently horizontal line of white lights aligned with green datum lights fixed on the sides of the mirror. The pilot could see by the lights whether he was too high, too low, or correct. The 'mirror' was adjustable, to give different flight approach paths for different aircraft, and gyro-stabilized, to compensate for the motion of the ship.

In 1952, forty-eight trial landings with optical landing aids were

Mirror landing sight device fitted to HMS *Albion*, September 1954

carried out by a Vampire on board *Illustrious*, and the 'Mirror' was introduced into service in 1954, the same year as the third important British flight deck innovation of the 1950s, the steam catapult. Fully-loaded modern aircraft could not take off without a catapult, but the hydraulic and compressed air catapults were reaching their design limits. Commander C. C. Mitchell RNVR conceived the idea of using steam from the ship's main boilers to operate the catapults. As finally developed by Brown Brothers of Edinburgh, the steam catapult gave power and to spare to launch any naval aircraft of the foreseeable future. It was fitted in *Perseus* in 1951, demonstrated to the US Navy in 1952; thenceforward Project 27C included the fitting of steam catapults. USS *Hancock*, the first US carrier to have the American C–11 steam catapult, began trials with it in June 1954. *Ark Royal*, commissioned in 1955, was the first British carrier to have the operational steam catapult. But she had only a $5\frac{1}{2}$ degree 'interim' angled deck whereas US carriers commissioning at that time had $10\frac{1}{2}$ degree angles.

Westland Whirlwinds, on their way to land troops at Port Said harbour, passing the statue of Ferdinand de Lesseps, builder of the Suez Canal

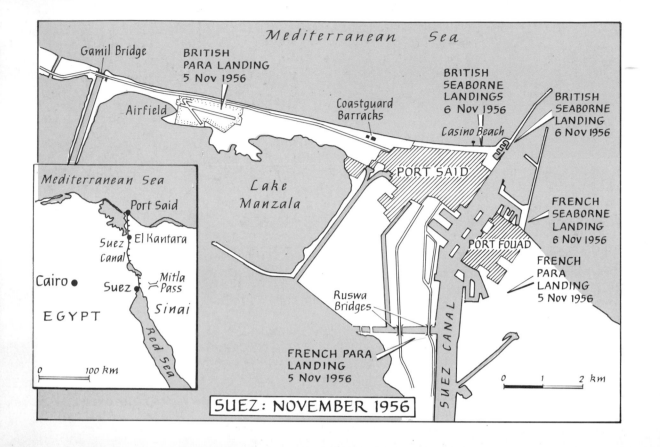

Mediterranean Sea

Gamil Bridge

BRITISH
PARA LANDING
5 Nov 1956

Airfield

Coastguard
Barracks

BRITISH
SEABORNE
LANDINGS
6 Nov 1956

Casino Beach

BRITISH
SEABORNE
LANDING
6 Nov 1956

PORT SAID

Lake
Manzala

FRENCH
SEABORNE
LANDING
6 Nov 1956

PORT FOUAD

FRENCH
PARA
LANDING
5 Nov 1956

Ruswa
Bridges

FRENCH PARA
LANDING
5 Nov 1956

SUEZ CANAL

0   1   2 km

SUEZ: NOVEMBER 1956

Mediterranean Sea

Port Said

Suez
Canal

El Kantara

Cairo

Suez

Mitla
Pass

EGYPT

Sinai

Red Sea

0   100 km

IN 1950, the United States, the United Kingdom and their allies had been broadly in agreement over their objective in Korea. The same was certainly not true in the Mediterranean in 1956, when President Nasser of Egypt nationalized the Suez Canal.

In July 1952, after a military coup, the corrupt, fun-loving King Farouk had abdicated in favour of his son. In June 1953, General Neguib deposed the infant King and became President. The real power, however, lay with Lieutenant Colonel Gamel Abdel Nasser, who was Prime Minister and then, in June 1956, President. Nasser was determinedly anti-Western. He antagonized the Americans by opposing the Baghdad Pact, the British by supporting Mau Mau in Kenya, and the French by supporting the Algerians. He was also, of course, implacably opposed to and increasingly hostile towards Israel. When, in 1956, first the Americans and the British, and then the Russians, withdrew promises of financial support for the building of the High Dam at Aswan, Nasser's eyes turned towards Egypt's only major source of income. On 26 July 1956, he combined financial expediency with personal satisfaction by taking over the Canal.

Had the United Kingdom and France, the two nations most affected, taken immediate military action, in a spirit of righteous retribution, world opinion would very probably have been on their side. But though the Mediterranean was a vital strategic area for the United Kingdom, and though the Suez Canal was crucial for the supply of oil from the Middle East, and even though the British Chiefs of Staff and the Cabinet met on 27 July and had actually put forward the idea of a military operation, the plain hard fact was that sufficient forces were not immediately available.

Eight infantry battalions, two battalions of paratroopers, and two battalions of Royal Marine Commandos were in Cyprus, engaged in operations against EOKA terrorists, which had seriously interfered with normal training: the Paras had done no parachute training, the Marines no amphibious training, for some time. In the event, considerable forces were used at Suez: on the British side, 45,000 men, 12,000 vehicles, 300 aircraft and 100 warships; on the French side, 34,000 men, 9,000 vehicles, 200 aircraft and 30 warships. But this force took time, literally months, to assemble. Cyprus would have to be the main base, although it had no deep-water harbour. Malta had Grand Harbour, but it was 1,000 miles from the Canal.

The Egyptian Navy was not a major force, having only four destroyers, some escort vessels and a dozen Soviet P.6 and five ex-British Fairmile MTBs. But the Egyptian Air Force was the largest in the Middle East, with several splendid airfields, taken over from the RAF under the Anglo-Egyptian Treaty of 1954, and some squadrons of modern Russian MiG–15s which outperformed all the RAF's and Fleet Air Arm's current fighters except the Hawker Hunters of No. 1 Squadron, at that time based in the United Kingdom.

Suez. HMS *Bulwark* (centre) steams past HMS *Eagle* (left) and HMS *Theseus* in Grand Harbour, Valetta, Malta. Foreground: The liner *Ascania* and the *Empire Cymric*

Westland Wyvern of 813
Squadron (see 'Dennis the
Menace' insignia) landing on
HMS *Eagle*

Of the British carriers, *Centaur* had been taken in hand for modernization. *Ark Royal* was at Devonport for an extended refit to cure the 'teething troubles' of her first commission. *Bulwark* was in home waters, as training and trials carrier. In a few hectic days, she was brought up to full complement, stored and ammunitioned for war, embarked three Sea Hawk squadrons, 804, 810 and 895, and arrived in Malta on 13 August. *Albion* was at Portsmouth, due to start working up in October. Her programme was hastened, so that she arrived in the Mediterranean on 17 September with two Sea Hawk squadrons, 800 and 802, 809 Sea Venoms and 'B' Flight of 849 Skyraiders.

The only British carrier in the Mediterranean in July was *Eagle*. Though a somewhat accident-prone vessel, she had been in commission since 1955 (setting up, on 23 August, the all-time British record of 201 sorties in a day) and had an all-purpose air group in a good state of training. As ground attack and army support were to be the main roles, her Gannet squadron, 812, was disembarked to Hal Far, Malta, and replaced by 893 Squadron Sea Venoms, which had been working up to join *Ark Royal*. Thus *Eagle* was to have two Sea Hawk squadrons, 897 and 899, two Sea Venom, 892 and 893, a Wyvern squadron, 830, and 'A' Flight of 849 Skyraiders.

The three carriers began an intensive work-up programme, based on Malta, with a visit to Toulon late in September for consultations and some flying exercises with the French Navy, which was to provide two carriers: *Arromanches* (ex-HMS *Colossus*, bought in 1951) with two squadrons, 14F and 15F, of F4U Corsairs, and *Lafayette* (formerly USS *Langley*) with one squadron, 9F, of Avengers.

In October, the training programme included helicopter drills. For Suez, the British carrier squadron, under Vice Admiral Sir Manley Power, flying his flag in *Eagle*, had two light fleet carriers:

Theseus, with the Whirlwind helicopters of 845 Squadron, and *Ocean*, with the Whirlwinds and Sycamores of the Joint (Army and RAF) Experimental Helicopter Unit (known as JEHU, although the 'experimental' was later dropped, to 'reassure the customers').

Operation MUSKETEER, the seizure of the Suez Canal, was to take place in three stages: air attacks by RAF aircraft from Cyprus and Malta, and by the carrier air groups off shore, to neutralize the Egyptian Air Force; an airborne landing by the British 16th Independent Parachute Brigade and the French 10th Airborne Division; and a sea-borne assault by the 3rd Commando Brigade, supported by one tank regiment of forty-eight Centurions. Later would come the British 3rd Infantry Division, sailing from the United Kingdom, and the French 7th Division Mécanique Rapide from Algeria.

Whilst political controversy began to rage, at home and at the United Nations, the carrier squadron continued to exercise for their roles in an operation which it seemed, by the end of October, was never going to arrive. But all doubts and boredom were dispelled on 29 October. At 5 pm Israeli paratroopers dropped at the eastern end of the Mitla Pass, the gateway into Sinai. During the night, Israeli armoured columns crossed the border into Egypt in two places and, a day later, in two more. Operation KADESH had begun.

The Air Attacks

The British and French governments denied any foreknowledge of the Israeli attacks, but their later excuses were unconvincing. At 8.30 am on that morning of 29 October, the three British carriers had slipped from their buoys in Grand Harbour and put to sea, ostensibly to take part in Exercise 'Boathook', but steaming east at ominously high speeds of over 20 knots.

When flying began, *Eagle* suffered a serious mishap when the main reaving wire of the starboard catapult broke during a launch and sent a Sea Hawk into the sea. The pilot, Lieutenant L.E. Middleton, of 897 Squadron, was rescued but the catapult was put out of action, beyond ship's staff's capacity to repair. All now depended upon the port catapult, which was known to be reaching the stage when its wires would have to be replaced – an eight-day task. Thus, from the very beginning of MUSKETEER, it was possible that the flagship with her large and balanced air group might not be able to operate her aircraft.

An ultimatum was issued to the Israeli and Egyptian governments, stating that British and French forces would occupy key positions on the Canal unless fighting ceased and the belligerents withdrew ten miles either side of the Canal. The Israelis, then many miles east of the Canal, agreed. The Egyptians did not, and the carriers therefore expected to fly off their first strikes at 4.30 am on the 31st, when the ultimatum expired.

But there was an anti-climactic delay, while the British and French carriers, with their screening ships, waited all day for the signal for action. When the sun went down on 31 October, the carriers' operations room plots began to show formations of radar contacts, at great heights, of RAF Canberras and Valiants from Cyprus and Malta on their way to bomb airfields in the Nile delta and along the Suez Canal.

The high-level bombing did very little damage, for the effort involved. Much more effective were the RAF Venoms and French F84F Thunderstreaks, from Akrotiri in Cyprus, attacking airfields in the Canal area, and the Sea Hawk and Sea Venom strikes flown off the carriers from early on 1 November. The first, of forty aircraft, attacked airfields at Cairo Almaza and Inchas, and at Cairo West where twelve Sea Hawks from *Bulwark* arrived ten minutes before sunrise. According to a contemporary account, 'every pilot tensed, concentrated on his own target. The Beagles (Russian-built bombers) and Lancasters took shape and grew larger beneath the fixed centre cross. Fire and fairy lights mottled the silver fuselages in the cold grey dawn. Suddenly a sheet of flame arched skywards etched with black billowing smoke.'

Several I1–28s and MiG–15s were destroyed on the ground by front-gun strafing. At this early stage, only pure jets were sent inland because air opposition was expected. But there was none, and only light flak. All aircraft returned safely to their carriers.

Later in the day, when the carriers had established a steady rhythm, turning into the wind and flying off fresh strikes every sixty-five minutes, attacks were extended to airfields at Bilbeis, Helwan and Heliopolis and the coastal airfield of Dekheila, near Alexandria, where turbo-prop Wyverns dive-bombed the runways. French Corsairs set on fire an Egyptian destroyer off Alexandria and sank an MTB (motor torpedo boat). In the Gulf of Suez, the cruiser HMS *Newfoundland* challenged and then sank the Egyptian frigate *Domiat*. The LST *Akka*, believed to be a block-ship, was bombed and rocketed at her moorings in Lake Timsah by Sea Hawks. Later, as the Egyptians were towing her into the Canal, she was bombed and hit again, but unfortunately she sank, partially blocking the main channel.

The next day, 2 November, began with strikes on airfields, but worthwhile targets were much harder to find and soon the Sea Hawks and Sea Venoms were down to smaller game, such as Harvard and Chipmunk trainers. By noon, all the main airfields had been bombed and strafed, some seventy aircraft destroyed and another ninety damaged, hangars had been set on fire, control towers wrecked and runways cratered. From photo-reconnaissance evidence and debriefing, it was decided that the Egyptian Air Force had been virtually eliminated. The Wyverns were allowed to fly further inland and the main target was a huge military transport depot, Huckstep Camp, east of Cairo, where there were over a thousand vehicles, including armour, parked in

Flak-damaged Sea Venom of 893 Squadron making 'wheels up' landing on HMS *Eagle*

neat rows in the open. These were worked over with bombs, rockets and 20 mm cannon shells.

Air opposition was non-existent, then and throughout MUS-KETEER, but the anti-aircraft gunners, as in Korea, improved with practice. During an attack on Almaza airfield, one of 893's Sea Venoms was hit by flak. The observer was injured and the hydraulic supply to the undercarriage severed. The pilot, Lieutenant Commander Wilcox, made a copy-book wheels-up landing on board *Eagle*, but his observer, Flying Officer Olding, later had his left leg amputated above the knee.

While *Albion* withdrew to refuel on 3 November, the other two carriers maintained the cycle of strikes, on airfields, Huckstep Camp again, an artillery barracks at Al Maya, and the large marshalling yard at Nefisha, near Ismalia, and made an armed reconnaissance of the Port Said–Ismalia road. French Corsairs dive-bombed Almaza and Dekheila, unfortunately losing one squadron commander. French F84F Thunderstreaks destroyed a radar station at Abu Sultan. Sub-Lieutenant C.J. Hall's Sea Hawk went over *Bulwark*'s side on landing and Hall was killed.

Above: Sea Hawk FB.3 of 897 Squadron flown by Lt L.E. Middleton from HMS *Eagle*, Mediterranean, 1956

Right: Attack by Sea Hawks and Wyverns from HMS *Eagle* on the Gamil Bridge

Eagle's air group took on Gamil Bridge, a solid causeway, west of Port Said, the coastal link to Alexandria. Sea Hawks and Wyverns dive-bombed it, but the bridge survived and the defenders shot down a Wyvern. The pilot, Lieutenant D.F. MacCarthy, used his ejection seat and came down in the sea only 4,000 yards from a hostile shore battery. Aircraft from *Eagle* and *Bulwark* maintained a defensive CAP overhead until a helicopter could arrive from *Eagle*, some seventy miles away. MacCarthy was eventually returned on board after two hours, unhurt.

Eagle's Sea Hawks returned to the bridge for a low level run, using delayed-action bombs, which they 'planted' in the side of the causeway like darts. After the delay, while the aircraft flew clear, the bombs detonated and blew away a third of the bridge.

On Sunday 4 November, *Eagle* retired to replenish with fuel and ammunition and fly on replacement aircraft from El Adem. During the day, a CAP from *Bulwark* sighted and strafed four Egyptian MTBs off Alexandria. A following strike with rockets blew up one MTB, set two others on fire and left the third damaged but able to pick up survivors. Restrictions on attacking Cairo International Airport, which had so far been 'out of bounds', were lifted to allow attacks on Il–28s and MiGs known to be there.

United States disapproval, personified by John Foster Dulles, of the Suez undertaking was by now making itself apparent at sea, where ships of the US Sixth Fleet were operating so close to the British that it seemed they were actually trying to impede the carriers. At one point, the British task force commander Admiral Durnford-Slater requested the American admiral to move on. He refused but did signal to Washington: 'Whose side am I on?' The US ships were showing lights at night. The British did the same so that (it was uncharitably said) any attacking Egyptian aircraft would have as good a chance of hitting American ships as British.

Airborne Assault on Port Said

Early on the morning of 5 November, three companies of the 3rd Battalion, the Parachute Regiment, were dropped on Gamil airfield from a flight of twenty-six Hastings and Valettas from Cyprus. 3 Para got down in ten minutes, with one man killed after landing in a minefield, and some casualties from small arms fire. They secured the airfield in about forty-five minutes and by 1 pm had cleared the area and were pressing on towards Port Said town.

Meanwhile, the French 2nd Colonial Parachute Regiment (RCP) dropped from Nord Noratlas aircraft on Port Fouad, opposite Port Said, and on the two Raswa bridges, south of Port Said. The RCP got down in their 'par' time of four minutes and, after some brief but fierce resistance, secured Port Fouad and one of the Raswa bridges, the second having already been blown.

Air cover was provided by 'cab ranks' of twelve to sixteen Sea Hawks and six Corsairs from the carriers. The French 'cab rank' was controlled by General Gilles, the airborne forces commander, who flew overhead for most of the day directing operations on the ground. Although the British carriers had never worked with the Parachute Brigade before, communications were very good. Pilots were briefed by R/T from the ground, using a co-ordinated fire plan, working over their allotted targets – some of them only one to two hundred yards ahead of the troops – for exactly nine and a half minutes.

Eagle lost another Wyvern during a strike on the Coastguard Barracks, on the western side of Port Said. It was a solid modern building, stoutly defended, which rocketing and dive-bombing had failed to subdue. The strike leader, Lieutenant Commander Cowling, placed his 1,000 lb delayed-action bomb precisely on the ground floor and gutted the building, but was hit and had to bale out using his ejection seat some ten miles out to sea. He was picked up by a helicopter which took him back to his ship.

That rescue helicopter had been supporting the paratroops on Gamil. About ninety minutes after the landing, the paratroops reported that they were short of wireless batteries and asked if the carriers could supply them. Batteries were flown in by helicopter, followed by medical supplies. Helicopters landed their stores, picked up wounded, and flew them out to the ships. A regular shuttle service was soon established between ships and shore, with the helicopters bringing in a doctor, and various stores and comforts, including a thousand gallons of fresh water in empty Bofors ammunition boxes, 'nutty' (chocolate), and cartons of cigarettes (Senior Service, naturally). They also evacuated thirty-seven wounded, including some French flown in from their landing area at Port Fouad.

A fourth company of 3 Para parachuted into Gamil that afternoon (there had not been room for them on the original lift), and the French dropped another battalion of 2 RCP. By that evening, after a possibility of a ceasefire which came to nothing, the Paras had consolidated in positions around the outskirts of Port Said. They had secured objectives in areas immediately forward of the beaches, where the assault forces were due to land early the next day. The town was virtually sealed off. The road to Suez was reported to be clear.

Assault from the Sea

By nightfall on 5 November, the invasion armada was on its way to Port Said, accompanied over the horizon by ships of the US Sixth Fleet and shadowed from a much closer but still discreet distance by the US submarines *Cutlass* and *Hardhead*. At 4 am on 6 November, carrier aircraft flew final strike sorties against Egyptian positions along the main beaches, after which an intense but controlled bombardment began, carried out by the cruisers and destroyers – the main armament of the French *Jean Bart*, the only battleship present, was not used.

A few miles off the coast, the invasion armada split into three, like the prongs of a trident. On the right, in their LSTs and with the HQ ship *Meon*, heading towards the Casino beach of Port Said, went 40 and 42 Commandos Royal Marines, and C Squadron 6 Royal Tank Regiment. To the left, towards Port Fouad, went the French 1st Foreign Legion Parachute Regiment, with a squadron of light AMX tanks. In the centre were assault ships carrying the rest of 16th Parachute Brigade and A Squadron of 6 RTR, due to land later in Port Said harbour itself.

Preceded by minesweepers on each wing, the invasion ships were approaching their objectives soon after 4 am. At 4.30 the bow doors of the LSTs opened and LVTs (landing vehicles, tracked),

Royal Marine Commandos
waiting to embark in helicopters
on board HMS *Theseus*

each with thirty men and their equipment, 'swam' to shore, landing 40 Commando to the left of the Casino Pier, and 42 Commando to the right. Fourteen Centurion tanks, specially waterproofed, came ashore beside the western breakwater. Harassed by some uncomfortably accurate sniper fire, but supported by the tanks and strikes by carrier aircraft (one of which unfortunately caused casualties to its own side) the Commandos began to fight their way through the streets of Port Said. The French got ashore without opposition, but were soon in action in Port Fouad, as they made progress towards the Raswa bridges, which were now under attack.

Meanwhile, 45 Commando had been waiting to land by helicopter from *Ocean* and *Theseus*, some seven miles offshore. After the first helicopter carrying the CO of 45 Commando, reconnoitring for a suitable landing place, had been hit but not discouraged, helicopters were approaching in waves by 6.30 to land their troops, under somewhat troublesome sniper fire, on a patch of waste ground beside De Lesseps' statue, near the Canal. Some of the

helicopters began to take back wounded at once. One Marine was hit, hauled back into the helicopter and was under treatment in *Ocean*'s sickbay only twenty minutes after leaving the ship.

The carriers flew constant 'cab rank' sorties over the beach-head during the day but had surprisingly few calls for assistance. Armed reconnaissances were flown along the Port Said–Ismalia road and *Eagle* lost another Sea Hawk during an attack on an army camp at El Kantara. The pilot, Lieutenant Donald Mills of 897 Squadron, ejected and landed in the desert on the eastern side of the Canal not far from El Kantara. British and French fighters flew a CAP over him until a helicopter could arrive from *Eagle*.

The whole of 45 Commando, some 425 men and 23 tons of stores, were brought ashore, faultlessly, in ninety minutes, in the first helicopter-borne assault landing in history. During the day, fourteen LSTs discharged troops, vehicles and stores ashore, either at Casino Wharf or in Port Said harbour. British and French troops linked at the Raswa bridge. Advance units had begun to probe southwards towards El Kantara and Ismalia. The leading Centurions were well on the way to Suez. There was no doubt that, after all the uncertainties, delays and changes of plan, Operation MUSKETEER was a success.

But the entire day had been beset by rumours. The men of the invasion force, when they could get a newspaper or listen to a news broadcast, had been greatly irritated by the quite preposterous media prominence given to the comparatively minute contribution of the RAF, and astonished by the seeming lack of interest in the Soviet invasion of Budapest, compared with the political hornets' nest Suez was stirring up at home and on the international front. There were reports of Soviet missiles on their way to the Middle East, and of Soviet submarines sighted off Alexandria. The Americans were selling sterling at knockdown prices. The Third World War was on the way – might even have started already.

There were also rumours, on this occasion true, of a ceasefire, which came into effect at 11 pm on the 6th, although the next day paratroopers were still digging in either side of the Canal, and there was still some street fighting and sniper fire in Port Said. By now, *Eagle*'s port catapult had made 631 launches and was looking 'frayed'. Admiral Power and his staff were transferred by helicopter to *Bulwark* on the afternoon of the 7th and *Eagle* left for Malta. For her, and indeed for everybody, the Suez venture was over, although there were some weary weeks of occupation of the Canal Zone and operations offshore still ahead.

The subsequent political uproar soon drowned the noise of battle. Whatever the politicians might say, MUSKETEER was reckoned a success by those who had to carry it out. The opinion of the men of the fleet, had they ever been consulted, was that whether or not it was wrong to begin the Suez operation, it was certainly wrong to end it prematurely.

Into the Sixties

WHILST the politicians who had themselves been largely responsible for it bemoaned the 'Suez débâcle', as it became known, the armed forces continued to regard it as a success and resented the political tendency to treat it as a self-inflicted injury. Nevertheless, Suez did cause a severe loss of national self-confidence and undoubtedly accelerated that retreat from Empire which was already under way, and which soon manifested itself in reduced resources for defence.

In 1957 Duncan Sandys published his White Paper, with a five-year Defence Plan. Conceding, in mitigation, that it was formulated under the shadow of the recently detonated hydrogen bomb, Sandys' 1957 White Paper still remains one of the quainter documents on defence ever published, even by a Conservative defence minister. It was, very broadly, it claimed, an acknowledgement that defence in a nuclear war was impossible. No important future role could be envisaged for manned aircraft. Fighter Command, for instance, would be limited to the defence of V-bomber and Thor missile bases. The V-bomber itself was eventually to be replaced by the Blue Streak rocket as the launch vehicle of the British deterrent. One of the more definite statements was that 'the role of naval forces in total war is uncertain'. It was allowed that 'carrier task forces' would still be needed, but the size of the Navy would be reduced.

In 1958, the concept of a balanced, all-purpose British fleet in European waters was abandoned. In their NATO context, aircraft carriers would have fighter and strike aircraft but would mostly be equipped with anti-submarine aircraft and helicopters. In June, it was announced that six carriers, *Unicorn*, *Warrior*, *Perseus*, *Theseus*, *Ocean* and *Glory*, were to be sold or scrapped. However, in January of that year, HMS *Victorious* commissioned, after an eight-year reconstruction. *Victorious* had been virtually rebuilt from the hangar deck up and now represented the latest Fleet Air Arm practice: two steam catapults, an $8\frac{3}{4}$ degree angled deck, and Type 984 computer-aided radar which gave a 'three-D' picture of surrounding contacts.

Her air group included the new Supermarine Scimitar fighter. This, the replacement for the Sea Hawk, was the FAA's first supersonic fighter (albeit Mach 1 was attained in a shallow dive). The Scimitar had two Rolls-Royce Avon 202 turbo-jets, each of 11,250 lbs static thrust; as the Americans said, 'Only the Limeys could make such a powerful aircraft go so slow.' The Scimitar was the first FAA aircraft to carry a nuclear weapon. The orthodox armament was four 30 mm guns, and bombs or missiles.

But, on 4 February 1958, barely three weeks after *Victorious*'s commissioning day, the keel was laid at Newport News, Virginia, of an aircraft carrier which would eclipse *Victorious* and indeed all preceding ships. USS *Enterprise* was 89,600 tons full load, was 1,040 feet long overall, had four shafts, eight pressurized-water nuclear reactors, a top speed of 33 knots, four C13 steam catapults, four

Grumman F–14 Tomcat being launched by steam catapult from USS *Enterprise* deck-edge lifts, and a total complement of nearly 6,000 officers and men. As first fitted she had neither guns nor missiles for self-defence, but she carried some ninety of a new generation of naval aircraft: the two-seat, twin turbo-jet, supersonic all-weather McDonnell F–4 Phantom II strike fighter; the single-seat, turbo-jet 900 mph Vought F–8 Crusader fighter; the single-seat Douglas A–4 Skyhawk, the successor to the Skyraider; and, later, the Grumman E–2 Hawkeye airborne warning aircraft. When she commissioned on 25 November 1961, the 'Big E' was not only the world's first nuclear-powered aircraft carrier, but the world's largest warship – and most expensive (estimated construction cost was $444 million).

Left: The Blackburn NA 39, prototype of the Buccaneer S1 low-level strike aircraft, being lowered into the hangar during trials in HMS *Victorious*, February 1960

Below: Supermarine Scimitar single-seat fighter landing on HMS *Ark Royal*. The Scimitar was the first Fleet Air Arm fighter capable of supersonic speeds and the first Fleet Air Arm aircraft to carry a nuclear weapon

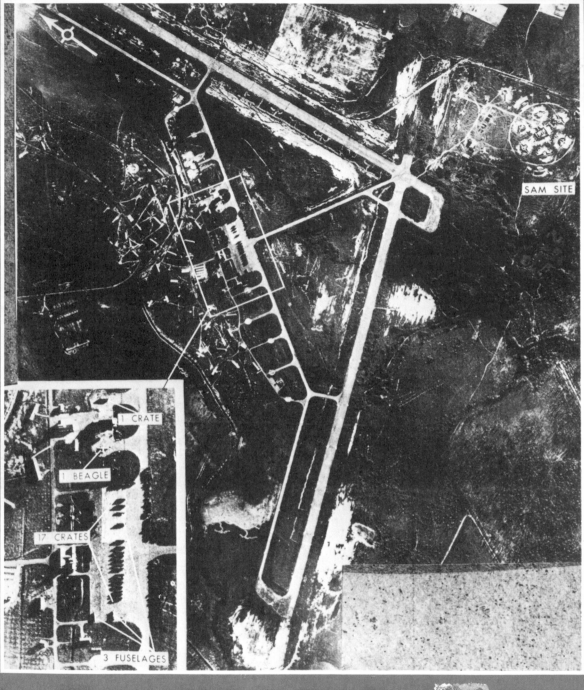

SAM SITE

1 CRATE

1 BEAGLE

17 CRATES

3 FUSELAGES

From the Lebanon to Cuba

IN the late 1950s and early 1960s, political coups and crises all over the world required the presence and quick response of sea power. On 14 July 1958, an armed revolt overthrew the pro-Western government of Iraq. The President of adjoining Lebanon, believing that the coup had been inspired by Nasser of Egypt, who had close links with the Soviet Union, and fearing that his own government would soon suffer a similar fate, asked for American assistance. In accordance with the Eisenhower Doctrine – that the United States would aid, if asked, any Middle Eastern government threatened by communism – the US Sixth Fleet, with three carriers and escorting cruisers and destroyers, arrived off the Lebanese coast on 15 July.

Covered by jets from the carriers, the first of an eventual 14,000 US Marines began to land from their amphibious ships on beaches near Beirut that afternoon. The British 16th Independent Parachute Brigade was flown into Amman, the capital of Jordan, the same day. With a degree of co-operation which had not been present at Suez, the Royal Navy's carriers also took part. *Eagle*'s air group flew covering sorties in the eastern Mediterranean. *Bulwark* took the 1st Battalion, the King's Own Regiment, from Mombasa to Aden, and then ferried the 1st Battalion, The Cameronians, up to Akaba. *Albion* brought 42 Commando Royal Marines out to Malta, and then steamed east to relieve *Eagle*, on station between the Lebanon and Cyprus. This rapid deployment of troops and air power stabilized the situation and, by October, the crisis had eased.

In August 1958, it was the turn of the US Seventh Fleet. The Chinese Communists had concentrated forces on the mainland

Above: US Marines landing at Beirut, July 1958

Opposite: Airfield in Cuba showing Russian IL–28 bombers and missile site

opposite the Nationalist-held islands of Quemoy and Matsu, only four miles off the coast of China. The Communists regarded these islands as their own, and as stepping stones to a conquest of Nationalist Taiwan. The Nationalists, for their part, saw the islands as launching pads for a return to the mainland.

When, on 23 August, the Communists bombed the islands, the five carriers of the Seventh Fleet had to assist the 100,000 Nationalists on the islands, but without becoming directly involved in a shooting war. This they accomplished by flying over Taiwanese air space, thus freeing Nationalist aircraft to engage the Communist MiGs, and by convoying amphibious tractors loaded with supplies from Taiwan to points close to the islands, from where they could make their own way in to shore. Once again, the crisis abated, as the Chinese turned to other preoccupations in Tibet and India.

Kuwait

In *Bulwark*'s busy commission, she not only ferried troops around the Middle East but steamed 52,000 miles and in the process salvaged a burning tanker in the Persian Gulf, earning her crew £100,000 – one of the largest salvage awards ever won by one of HM ships. On paying off early in 1959, *Bulwark* was taken in hand at Portsmouth for conversion into what was ploddingly called in officialese an LPH (landing platform helicopter), better known as a Commando carrier.

This was one of the lessons learned from the successes of *Ocean* and *Theseus* and their helicopters at Suez. Clearly, in what seemed to be an endemically unstable world political situation, there was an important role for carriers specially equipped to land troops rapidly by helicopter at trouble spots.

Bulwark's guns, radar, radio equipment and fighter direction capability were retained, but her catapults and arrester wires were removed. Gantries to carry four assault landing craft were built on her sides. Her messdecks, store rooms and magazines were converted to accommodate a complete Royal Marine Commando of some 600 officers and men, with their arms, stores and vehicles. A Fleet Air Arm helicopter squadron was embarked, to land the Marines initially and also to operate tactically in the field. The ship was air-conditioned, to be able to operate anywhere from the Arctic to the tropics.

Bulwark commissioned in January 1960 to carry 42 Commando, and embarked 848 Squadron, of sixteen Westland Whirlwinds, with five in reserve, in March. (Her sister ship *Albion* was similarly converted a year later, completing in the summer of 1962.) *Bulwark* sailed for the Mediterranean and the Far East. Her new role was put to an operational test in July 1961. Major General Abdul Kassem, head of a military junta which had seized power in Iraq, claimed sovereignty over the state of Kuwait, on the

Persian Gulf. The Ruler of Kuwait asked for British assistance.

Buccaneer launch

Bulwark, about to visit Karachi, sailed 'with all dispatch' and within twenty-four hours 848 Squadron was landing 42 Commando in air temperatures rising to 124 degrees and a 30-knot wind which whipped up violent sandstorms reducing visibility to less than a quarter of a mile. After initial uncertainty, Kuwait airfield was found, by bearings provided from the ship and some 'enlightened guesswork' on the part of 848's CO. Supplied and supported by 848, the Marines secured the airfield and dug themselves in. 45 Commando was flown in from Aden by the RAF the next day, and a build-up to a balanced force of some 5,700 men was completed in nine days.

Victorious, which had been at Hong Kong on 29 June, reached Bahrain in ten days and, with her large air group and Type 984 radar, took charge of air defence (including control of RAF Hunters flying from Kuwait) while flying anti-submarine and airborne early warning patrols out to sea.

By September, although Kassem continued to issue vague threats to 'liberate' Kuwait, the crisis had subsided. Once again, a balanced and sufficient force, with its own air cover, had been assembled and landed where it was needed.

A medium-range ballistic missile base in Cuba with four launchers and equipment

Cuba

On 17 April 1961, the carrier *Essex* was standing by to give air cover, had President Kennedy authorized it, to the Bay of Pigs landing. The President did not do so. A famous fiasco ensued. American prestige worldwide was seriously damaged, and Cuba was driven even further into the arms of Soviet Russia.

In the summer of 1962, American intelligence reported an ominous number of Soviet ships arriving in Cuba with men, weapons, fighters and surface-to-air missiles. On 14 October, a high-flying U2 reconnaissance aircraft photographed what were identified as sites for long-range missiles – only a hundred miles from the United States.

Kennedy decided upon a sea and air blockade, or 'quarantine', as he called it. The US Air Force put four tactical squadrons, and all inter-continental ballistic missile crews, on alert. Thousands of troops were moved to embarkation points in Florida and Georgia. The US Navy formed Task Force 136, of seventeen destroyers and two cruisers, supported by carrier aircraft, to enforce the immediate quarantine. In all, 480 ships, and almost 400,000 military personnel, were to be involved.

On 22 October 1962, the President went on television to inform

the country and the world that Soviet Russia had placed offensive missiles in Cuba. Cuba would be quarantined until the missiles were removed. If the Soviets had not by then shown signs of dismantling the missile sites and halting the arms build-up, a naval blockade would begin in thirty-six hours' time, at 9 am on the 24th.

A quarantine line was established 500 miles north-east of Cuba. US aircraft, particularly carrier-borne FR–8A Crusaders, flew day and night surveillance flights overhead. Six Soviet ships were reported to have stopped or turned back, and Secretary of State Dean Rusk said 'we're eyeball to eyeball and I think the other fellow just blinked'. But by 25 October, other Soviet ships were continuing their voyages. Next day, a Panamian-owned ship, under charter to the Soviets, was stopped and searched for weapons or proscribed cargo. None was found and she was allowed to proceed.

By 27 October, it seemed that the world was on the very brink of a nuclear war. But, on the 28th, Nikita Khrushchev announced that the missiles would be withdrawn from Cuba, under UN supervision, if Kennedy agreed not to invade Cuba – some 30,000 US Marines were at that moment embarked and waiting offshore. Kennedy responded. Although American forces remained on alert for another three weeks, the crisis had been resolved.

The Soviet ship *Kasimov* under way to Cuba with fifteen IL–28 fuselages in crates on the upper deck

Confrontation

IN the 1960s, the Royal Navy was frequently involved in the political backwash and counter-currents of the receding tide of Empire. In March 1958, the last Flag Officer, Malaya, had hauled down his flag at Singapore, after the formation of the Federation of Malaya, which was to have included Brunei, whose Sultan had accepted the principle of federation.

But on 8 December 1962, an armed revolt by the 'North Borneo Liberation Army', who were opposed to the Federation, broke out in Brunei, and in nearby Sarawak and North Borneo. The Sultan appealed for British help. An advance party of 42 Commando Royal Marines was flown in from Singapore. In a daring sortie, one company rescued the resident and European nationals who were held as hostages in the coastal town of Limbang. The Commando carrier *Albion*, on passage from Mombasa with 40 Commando on board, steamed to Singapore at top speed, embarked HQ 3 Commando Brigade and sailed for Labuan. 40 Commando were landed by helicopter and coastal craft at Kuching in Sarawak and were then flown to Brunei to join 42 Commando.

Later, the cruiser *Tiger*, destroyers, frigates, minesweepers and tank landing craft brought up more troops and fire power. Supported by the helicopters from sea, while the minesweepers patrolled the coasts, the Commandos had the situation under control in a week. All the major towns in Brunei and Sarawak were cleared of rebels by February 1963.

Unfortunately, this was only the beginning of what became known as 'confrontation', which was nothing less than an undeclared war, deliberately played down in the media by both sides, so that few who did not take part in it were ever aware of its duration or extent.

In September 1963, a new independent State of Malaysia was proclaimed, formed from the Federation of Malaya, the State of Singapore, British North Borneo (renamed Sabah), and Sarawak – but without Brunei, chiefly because of a failure to reach an agreement over the Sultanate's oil revenues.

The new Federation was violently opposed in Indonesia, whose President Sukarno had openly sympathized with, and covertly supported, the North Borneo Liberation Army. Sukarno refused to recognize the State of Malaysia, and threatened a 'terrible confrontation'. In Indonesia there was the familiar pattern of anti-British riots, the burning of the British Embassy in Jakarta and looting of British citizens' homes and property. Malaysia, which Sukarno had promised to 'crush before the sun rose on 1 January 1965', broke off diplomatic relations with Indonesia.

Indonesian guerrilla attacks and infiltrations began to increase along the 970-mile border between Malaysian Sarawak and Indonesian Borneo, known as Kalimantan. Surveillance and operations on this border, which ran through thick jungle and had never been accurately mapped, was the task of a small British Security Force, commanded by Major General Walter C. Walker – with the traditional help from the Navy.

Westland Whirlwind of 848 Squadron operating in support of troops in Malaya

Once again, naval helicopters swung into their roles, familiar from Malaya a decade earlier, of supporting and transporting the troops ashore. Their flying effort, over the most difficult jungle terrain, often through torrential rainstorms, with inadequate maps, radar and radio aids, and weather forecasts, was truly prodigious: in 1963, 846 Squadron Westland Whirlwinds flew 3,750 operational sorties and won that year's Boyd Trophy. The Trophy for 1964 went to 845 Squadron, whose Westland Wessexes (bigger and more powerful than the Whirlwinds) flew 10,000 operational hours, transported 50,000 passengers, evacuated 500 casualties, and ferried millions of pounds of ammunition and stores.

The helicopters' normal bases were their carriers, *Albion* and *Bulwark*, but they also flew from a small airfield ashore at Sibu – named HMS *Hornbill*, after the national bird – and from a forward base at Nanga Gaat, 150 miles inland and only 30 miles from the Indonesian border.

Nanga Gaat was the home of the Iban tribe, who very quickly established a close and warm relationship with the helicopter crews. Squadron personnel lived in Iban 'long huts', wore sarongs and bead necklaces in the evenings, and some learned to speak the Iban language. One prominent Iban adopted a Marine helicopter pilot as his son, and a young Iban mother, flown by helicopter to hospital for a difficult childbirth, named the resulting son Helicopter Anak Manjan.

Confrontation ended in 1966 with the signing of an agreement, after the ousting of Sukarno. The last British force, appropriately 40 Commando, withdrew in September. But the contribution of the helicopters, and of fixed-wing aircraft from *Victorious*, operating for prolonged periods, not only in Borneo but along the coasts of Malaya itself, was and still remains very largely unsung.

'Brush fires' continued to break out all over what had been the British Empire. In 1964, there were mutinies in the armies of the newly independent countries of Uganda and Kenya, and in Tanzania (formerly Tanganyika) where President Nyerere asked for British help. *Albion*, leaving most of her helicopters behind in Borneo, steamed towards the African coast. *Victorious* was also available. *Centaur* embarked 500 men of 45 Commando and their equipment at Aden and landed them by helicopter on 24 January at Dar-es-Salaam to restore order, which they did in a week.

In May 1964, after an armed insurrection by tribesmen in the Radfan mountains, north of Aden, 815 Squadron's Wessex from *Centaur* lifted 45 Commando into the Radfan area; four Wessex carried nearly 550 men and their equipment in one day. Helicopters from *Albion*, flying from the ship or from RAF Khormaksar, supported units of 45 Commando and the Federal Army up country, and also assisted the security forces to combat terrorists in Aden itself. When law and order broke down in British Guiana the same year, troops were flown in from the United Kingdom, and

Marines were landed from the frigate *Whirlwind*. Helicopters lifted the troops to trouble spots in the countryside.

In September and October 1965, *Eagle*'s aircraft assisted the local forces in Aden. In 1966, *Eagle* and *Ark Royal* in turn patrolled the Mozambique Channel, to enforce the United Nations oil embargo on Rhodesia. In this 'Beira Blockade', *Eagle* spent seventy-one days continuously at sea, and in a patrol of forty-four days her Sea Vixens, Buccaneers, Scimitars and Gannets flew over 1,000 sorties, identified 770 ships, gave surveillance over 200,000 square miles a day, and covered more than half a million miles in 2,000 flying hours.

As the decade went on, it seemed that the only conflict in which the Royal Navy's carriers were not involved – and profoundly grateful they were for it – was the seemingly bottomless quagmire of Vietnam.

'The Well', the only prepared helicopter landing spot on the River Balui, north of Belaga, Indonesia, October 1963

Vietnam

Dien Bien Phu, November 1953

THE Vietnamese were struggling to achieve national independence as far back as the third century AD, when Trieu Au, the Vietnamese Joan of Arc, led a revolt against China and, being gloriously defeated at the age of twenty-three, committed suicide. Thus the French, who assaulted Tourane (Da Nang) in 1858 and occupied Saigon a year later, and the Japanese, who drove out the French in 1940, were only the latest in a long line of invaders.

During the Second World War, Ho Chi Minh (meaning 'He Who Enlightens') created the Vietnam Independence League, otherwise known as the Vietminh, to bring about Vietnamese independence, under a communist regime. At the Potsdam Conference in July 1945, Allied leaders decided to disarm the Japanese in Vietnam by the British in the south and the Chinese Nationalists in the north. British forces arrived in Saigon on 13 September and soon returned authority to the French, although for some time after the war the Japanese retained their arms because there were no other forces available to keep order.

On 2 September 1945, Ho Chi Minh declared the independence of Vietnam. Negotiations with the French broke down at Fontainebleau in September 1946. Amidst heightening political tension in November and December, French warships bombarded the port of Haiphong, and the Vietminh attacked French garrisons. The Vietminh withdrew from Hanoi in December 1946, and Ho Chi Minh and his supporters took to the countryside. The civil war had begun, which was to last for the next thirty years.

Dien Bien Phu

In Indo-China, the French suffered from a chronic shortage of aircraft and, equally seriously, from a lack of knowledge of how aircraft should be properly used. France had been defeated very early in the Second World War and now had no senior officers with experience of air command at a high level. Neither the Navy nor the Air Force was consulted over the conduct of the war in Indo-China. Aircraft were always requested on a piecemeal basis and each ground commander tended to acquire his own personal air force.

Nevertheless, the French aircraft carriers played their parts. The aged *Béarn* ferried aircraft out to Indo-China, arriving in Saigon in March 1946. Later in the year she took troops north for an assault on Haiphong. The escort carrier *Dixmude* (ex-HMS *Biter*) arrived from France in March 1947 and operated her Douglas SBD Dauntless dive-bombers off the Vietnamese coast until May. In October, her aircraft flew more than 200 sorties and dropped 65 tons of bombs in support of a French paratroop landing north of Hanoi.

HMS *Colossus*, loaned to the French in 1945 and renamed *Arromanches* (and finally bought by the French in 1951), relieved *Dixmude* in November 1948. She steamed up the Saigon river (the largest ship to do so) and disembarked her Seafire IIIs and *Dixmude*'s Dauntlesses to operate ashore for a period. *Dixmude* ferried a shipload of Grumman F6F Hellcats and Curtiss SB2C Helldivers from the United States. *Arromanches* took over these aircraft and operated for seven months off the coast, flying more than 670 sorties in support of the French troops ashore.

Arromanches shuttled back and forth, bringing replacement aircraft from France. In June 1951, *Lafayette* (ex-USS *Langley*) arrived to operate her Hellcats and Helldivers alongside *Arromanches*. A third carrier, *Bois Belleau* (ex-USS *Belleau Wood*), loaned by the United States but manned by the French, joined in April 1954.

The precise reason for occupying Dien Bien Phu, a remote village in northern Vietnam near the Laotian border, was never made clear even within the French high command. It was, depending upon who was speaking, to be an air-supplied 'hedgehog', to make life prickly for the Vietminh, or a large patrol base or 'mooring point', to stabilize the tactical situation in the north, or a 'preventive action' against another Vietminh drive into Laos.

But whatever the reason for their jump, the first French paratroops who landed in drop zone 'Natasha', a few hundred yards north-west of Dien Bien Phu, on the morning of 20 November 1953, soon discovered that the Vietnamese army commander General Vo Nguyen Giap was able to muster more troops and artillery to threaten Dien Bien Phu, and in time to besiege and take it, than the French would ever have believed possible. In a very few weeks, there was no question of the 15,000 French soldiers and legionaires in Dien Bien Phu going on the offensive. On the contrary, theirs became a fight to survive where they stood.

The French naval air arm did its best to avert the débâcle at Dien Bien Phu, which was nearly 200 miles from the sea. In the 167-day siege, 10,400 sorties were flown, 6,700 for supply or troop transport, and 3,700 combat sorties– of those, 1,267 by the French Navy, flying Helldivers of 3 Squadron and Hellcats of 11 Squadron, from *Arromanches*, a squadron of F8F Bearcats, and, towards the end, Corsairs from *Bois Belleau*. The French Navy also had six Privateer bombers of 28 Squadron, for deep penetration.

The naval aircraft flew along the 'Flak corridors' above the roads leading to beleaguered Dien Bien Phu, strafing coolie columns and the rare truck. Targets became harder to find as the Vietminh, adept at camouflage, even tied the tops of palms together to conceal traffic. The flak increased daily in accuracy and volume. Lieutenant Andrieux, CO of 3 Squadron, was shot down on 31 March, he and his crewman being killed. On 15 April, a nervous naval pilot, under fire and anxious to get away, dropped an intelligence pouch outside the defensive perimeter; priceless photographs, codebooks, and details of future French plans fell into Vietminh hands.

When *Belleau Wood* arrived in April 1954, the pilots of 11 Squadron, who were supposed to join her, had all been hit by flak or made at least one crash landing. Six had been shot down, with three killed and one taken prisoner. They had, as Captain Patou of *Arromanches* said, 'reached the limit of physical and nervous wear and tear', and were withdrawn.

On 7 May 1954, when the red Vietminh flag was flying over the French command posts in Dien Bien Phu, the US carriers *Essex* and *Boxer* were in the South China Sea, their flight decks crowded with aircraft, waiting, as they had been for some time, to fly off strikes in support of the beleaguered garrison. But despite French appeals, President Eisenhower refused to sanction American intervention. The United States had just finished a three-year war in Korea and, moreover, Eisenhower was quite rightly reluctant to risk an escalation which might bring Russia or China into Vietnam.

The eight-man crew of a Navy Privateer, shot down on 7 May, were the last Frenchmen killed in combat in Dien Bien Phu. During the siege, the French suffered some 10,000 casualties, including 2,000 dead. The 9,000 survivors were forced on a 'death march' to prison camps, from which less than a third returned.

Curtiss Hell Diver on the catapult of the French aircraft carrier *Bois Belleau*

Incident in the Gulf of Tonkin

The disaster at Dien Bien Phu, a shattering blow to the prestige and self-confidence of the French Army and to the French government's will to persevere in Indo-China, led to the end of French rule. Talks between the French and the Vietminh government of Ho Chi Minh began in Geneva on 8 May 1954. As a result, Vietnam was partitioned into North and South, with a Demilitarized Zone (DMZ) along the 17th Parallel.

Broadly, the political situation was to develop in a way very similar to that in Korea, with a communist government in the north and the American-backed, non-communist government of Emperor Bao Dai and his Prime Minister Ngo Dinh Diem in the south, both claiming – and, in the case of the communists, intending to achieve – sovereignty over the whole country.

There was never any long-term overall plan for the increasing American involvement in the politics and the armed forces of South Vietnam. Events followed each other in a seemingly inevitable progression. In 1955, the US Navy began on the humanitarian task of Operation PASSAGE TO FREEDOM, in which 900,000 North Vietnamese, most of them Catholics, were resettled in the south. In 1956, the French withdrew, and a US Military Assistance Advisory Group took over the training of the ARVN (South Vietnamese Army). In 1959, the communists in the north decided to overthrow the Diem government by force of arms. South Vietnamese communists, now known as the Viet Cong, organized massed demonstrations, and attacked government posts and buildings, and units of the ARVN.

In 1960, there were 875 US military personnel in South Vietnam. By 1964, when both Diem and President Kennedy had been murdered, the number had increased to 23,310. American deaths in action had risen from 1 in 1961 to 137 in 1964. Although the US Navy maintained a carrier force off Vietnam, the only flights over Vietnamese territory were photographic reconnaissance sorties, which provided invaluable information about communist activites without provoking communist reaction.

So matters might have continued. But on the night of 31 July 1964, South Vietnamese assault boats carried out a hit-and-run raid on some North Vietnamese islands. Thirty-six hours later, on the night of 2 August, the US destroyer *Maddox* was some ten miles off the coast of North Vietnam (within what the Vietnamese claimed as territorial waters). *Maddox* was just passing Hon Me Island, thirty miles south of the North Vietnamese PT (patrol torpedo) boat base at Loc Chao, when her radar screens showed three high-speed targets approaching.

The three North Vietnamese PT boats stood on, after a warning shot from *Maddox*, and two fired torpedoes. Both missed, and there was an exchange of fire after which the attackers withdrew, with damage to one of them. Four F8E Crusader fighters from the

The shadow of a US Navy photo reconnaissance aircraft over a burning North Vietnamese PT boat – one of five destroyed by aircraft from USS *Midway* and *Hancock*, May 1965

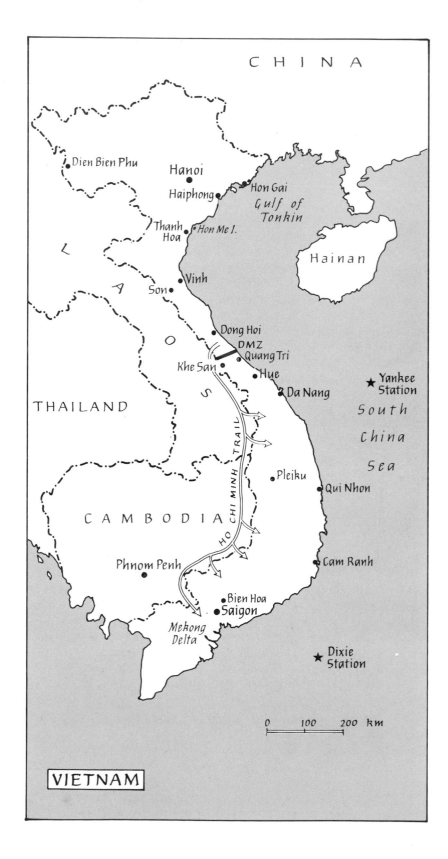

VIETNAM

carrier *Ticonderoga*, already in the air, were directed to the area and made several strafing runs with 20 mm cannon and Zuni unguided rockets. One PT boat was badly damaged and later sank.

Maddox resumed her patrol, with another destroyer, the *C. Turner Joy*, and on the night of 4/5 August suffered what was thought to be a second torpedo attack, by five suspicious radar contacts, which the destroyers engaged with gunfire at a range of 6,000 yards.

After two such attacks on American warships, President Johnson ordered air strikes in retaliation. Although the weather had been unsettled and *Maddox*'s captain later signalled his doubts about the authenticity of the second attack, the air strikes went ahead. *Ticonderoga* and *Constellation* launched sixty-four aircraft, F8 Crusaders, A–1 Skyraiders and A–4 Skyhawks, to bomb and rocket North Vietnamese naval bases from Quang Khe, fifty miles north of the DMZ, to Hon Gai in the north. An oil storage depot at Vinh was set on fire, and hits were claimed on twenty-nine ships.

'It was sort of like a dream,' said Lieutenant Everett Alvarez, one of the first to be launched from *Constellation*. 'We were actually going to war, into combat. I never thought it would happen, but all of a sudden here we were, and I was in it.' Alvarez's A–4C Skyhawk was hit over Hon Gai. 'I was very low, just skimming the trees at about five hundred knots. Then I had the weirdest feeling. My airplane was hit and started to fall apart, rolling and burning. I knew I wouldn't live if I stayed with the airplane, so I ejected, and luckily I cleared a cliff.'

Alvarez was captured and became the first American prisoner-of-war in Vietnam. It was to be eight and a half years before he was released, in 1973.

'Flaming Dart'

The incident in the Gulf of Tonkin was trivial, and it is still arguable whether North Vietnamese aggression, or South Vietnamese provocation, aided by the United States, was chiefly responsible. But it had one important consequence: in an atmosphere of alarm and indignation at such attacks on American ships, what became known as the 'Gulf of Tonkin Resolution' was rushed through Congress and, despite the misgivings of some Congressmen, signed by President Johnson on 11 August 1964. In effect, it gave the President authority to use American armed force in Vietnam.

Off Vietnam, the ships and men of Task Force 77 (the same designation as in Korea over a decade earlier) prepared for action. *Ticonderoga* and *Constellation* were joined by a third attack carrier, *Ranger*, and the anti-submarine carrier *Kearsarge* to guard against possible Chinese submarine activity.

F8 Crusaders equipped with air-intercept radar, and armed with Sidewinder air-to-air missiles, 20 mm cannon, and Zuni rockets for flak suppression, flew CAPs over intelligence-gathering ships, known as De Soto patrols, close to the Vietnamese coast. But there was little other action until 7 February 1965, when the Viet Cong attacked a US compound in the Central Highlands. Nine Americans were killed, and 100 wounded.

Once again, in a spirit of outrage, retaliatory strikes codenamed FLAMING DART were launched the same day, of forty-nine aircraft from *Coral Sea* and *Hancock*, and thirty-four aircraft from *Ranger*, against barracks north of the DMZ. A South Vietnamese strike was led by no less a pilot than General Ky, the Air Force commander.

The Viet Cong responded with further attacks on 10 February, killing twenty-three US soldiers and wounding many more. These again provoked a same-day strike (FLAMING DART II) of ninety-nine aircraft from the same three carriers against another barracks, at Chanh Hoa, thirty-five miles north of the DMZ. These were known as Alpha strikes, because they included all available aircraft, from fighters to tankers, of a carrier's air wing.

Carrier operations were constantly hindered by the north-east monsoon, which blows in the South China Sea from November until April, bringing heavy cloud, rain and low visibility. But in any case the Viet Cong seemed unimpressed by carrier strikes, whether Alpha or not, and continued their attacks on US personnel and installations. The President decided that a further escalation of the war was necessary.

'Rolling Thunder'

The United States' aim in South Vietnam was the same as it had been in South Korea: the establishment of a stable regime, capable of dealing with internal unrest and of defending itself against attack, especially from the north. There were many resemblances to Korea. For instance, the thinking behind Operation RANCH HAND in 1961, when large tracts of land across Vietnam were defoliated by Agent Orange sprayed from the air, in an attempt to prevent free movement across country by the Viet Cong, had resonances of the long air campaign to 'strangle' the North Korean supply line from Manchuria.

But there were many crucial differences. The government in South Vietnam was unstable and corrupt and, with its own curious combination of autocracy and feebleness, became even less stable after Diem's death. The communists controlled large parts of the South Vietnamese countryside to an extent they never did in Korea. The UN navies had blockaded the sea on either side of Korea. But the North Vietnamese could reinforce the Viet Cong through the Ho Chi Min trail in neighbouring Laos.

The United States had never lost a war and was not about to start now. Thus the Americans neglected the study of methods of waging war other than the application of force, and even the force they did apply was often applied too late. Above all, the Americans totally underestimated the losses the North Vietnamese were prepared to endure, and the determination of their leaders to go on until they won.

But in 1965, the year of greatest escalation of the war, all these revelations lay in the future. On 2 March, a bombing campaign began, code-named ROLLING THUNDER. Its object was literally to roll the war up into the north, in the expectation that the North Vietnamese would sue for peace before it reached Hanoi. (In fact, it was to last until 1 November 1968, when President Johnson halted all air attacks in exchange for North Vietnamese agreement to begin peace talks in Paris.)

On 8 March, 3,500 US Marines landed at Da Nang, to reinforce the city's defences, and on 7 May another 1,400 Marines and Sea Bees landed at Chu Lai, fifty miles south of Da Nang, to build an airfield there for ground support. In July, the decision was taken to commit 125,000 American combat ground troops to Vietnam.

For Task Force 77, ROLLING THUNDER began on 18 March with strikes from *Coral Sea* and *Hancock* against supply buildings at Phu Van and Vinh Son, and continued up and down the North Vietnamese coast to within seventy miles of Hanoi. In those early days, General Westmoreland, the US Military Assistance Com-

Defoliant spraying over North Vietnam

mander in Vietnam, lacked enough airfields for ground support, and relied upon naval assistance – so much so that by June 1965, five attack carriers were on station in the South China Sea.

Casualties to flak, light at first, began to increase ominously. But, to their consternation, carrier air wings found they could not take proper counter-measures without political approval.

For example, the first surface-to-air missile (SAM) site was photographed and identified, fifteen miles south-east of Hanoi, on 5 April. The SAM sites soon began to multiply. But it was not until 12 August, when several aircraft, including A–4 Skyhawks from *Midway*, had been lost that an anti-SAM operation, IRON HAND, was authorized. Even then, the first SAM site was not actually attacked until 17 October.

ROLLING THUNDER was conducted under the strictest political control. President Johnson was determined that the campaign should not escalate to the threshold of nuclear war and kept a tight grip upon events. No strike could be flown without approval from Washington; some targets, it was said, had to be approved by the President himself. If a strike was cancelled, because of the weather or any other reason, approval had to be obtained all over again.

No follow-up secondary strikes were allowed. Air-to-air combat was not permitted unless the enemy aircraft had been positively identified. Unexpended bombs or rockets could not be used against targets of opportunity. They had to be jettisoned into the sea before returning to the carriers.

No pre-strike photography was allowed: photographic reconnaissance aircraft had either to fly with the strike, or follow it immediately afterwards. This led to predictable losses in the reconnaissance squadrons. The gunners on the ground soon learned that, after the main strike had left, a solitary photographic aircraft would appear overhead.

The SA–2 Guideline SAMs, which were 35-foot, two-stage rockets with a 349 lb high-explosive warhead and an operational ceiling of just under 60,000 feet, were not the only hazard. Extra early-warning radar sites were installed. The number of anti-aircraft guns, many of them radar-controlled and directed, doubled and redoubled until some of the older pilots said that the flak over North Vietnam was more intense and dangerous than anything they had ever experienced over Germany in the Second World War.

The MiG–17 (a development of the MiG–15 of Korean days) made its first combat appearance, south of Hanoi, on 3 April 1965. On 17 June, two Phantom F–4Bs (much faster but less handy than the MiG–17) of VF–21 from *Midway* made the first MiG kills of the war, shooting down two MiG–17s with their Sparrow missiles. This was very encouraging, especially as the Secretary of the Navy, Paul H. Nitze, was on board *Midway* at the time. But the ratio of kills to losses was still unfavourable. There was every sign this was going to be a long and a hard war.

More, More, More...Aircraft and Carriers

When the carrier *Independence* arrived in the Gulf of Tonkin in June 1965, her air wing included one squadron (VA–75, the 'Sunday Punchers') of the new twin-engined, two-seater Grumman A–6A Intruder all-weather attack bombers, which replaced the A–3B Skywarrior in the US Navy. An odd-looking aircraft, variously described as a frying pan or a tadpole, the Intruder nevertheless had a maximum speed of 644 mph, and a ceiling of 42,400 feet, could carry a weapons load of 18,000 lbs, and had a marvellous array of electronic systems to identify and attack its targets, centred on an extensive avionics suite of digital integrated attack and navigational equipment (DIANE).

Anxious eyes watched these multi-million dollar packages of fabulous computers and electronic marvels take off for their first sorties over Vietnam. But the Intruder was an immediate success. The A–1 Skyraiders and A–4 Skyhawks, successful though they were, needed clear weather. The Intruder could locate targets, flying over any terrain, at low altitude, by day or night, and in any weather, including the north-eastern monsoon. Its hitting power was so great that in April 1966 Radio Hanoi proclaimed indignantly that the Americans were using B–52 Stratofortresses against population centres. In fact, the raid complained of had been made on the Uong Bi power plant, by just two Intruders of VA–85 'Black Falcons' from *Kitty Hawk* who each dropped thirteen 1,000 lb bombs.

Also embarked in *Kitty Hawk*, which had arrived in November 1965, was another strange-looking newcomer, the Grumman E–2A Hawkeye airborne early warning aircraft. The Hawkeye had twin turbo-prop engines, four vertical stabilizers, and a most striking 24-foot-diameter radome (rotating at 6 rpm) mounted on top of the fuselage. The Hawkeye's task was long-range airborne surveillance, but with a crew of two pilots and three or four systems operators it could also act as an aerial command and communication centre for fighter direction and control of bomber strikes.

The most successful carrier-borne aircraft to make its combat debut over Vietnam was the McDonnell Douglas F–4 Phantom II, which first became operational with the US Navy in December 1960. It was indeed so successful that the US Air Force equipped many squadrons with their own version, the F–4E. With a speed over Mach 2, more than 1,400 mph, and a weapons load of 15,000 lbs, the Phantom fulfilled a wider variety of roles than any other aircraft in Vietnam: tactical ground strike, close air support for ground troops, long-range interdiction, flak suppression, and reconnaissance, as well as air-to-air combat in which it became the 'MiG killer', destroying 146 MiGs in Vietnam (38 by the Navy, and 108 by the Air Force).

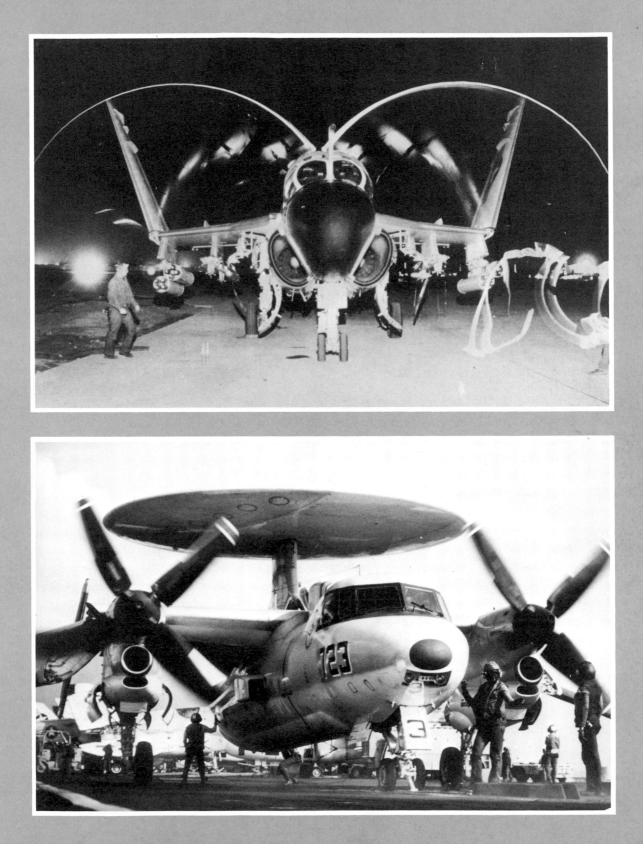

When a carrier first arrived off Vietnam, she normally operated for a short time at 'Dixie' station, in the South China Sea, about 115 miles south-east of Cam Ranh Bay. The southern war zone was less intense. At Dixie, new carriers and their air wings had a 'work-up' period in which to practise their flight deck drills, accustom themselves to the common round and daily task of launching and recovering sorties, sharpen their skills at interception, bombing and strafing, and generally become acclimatized to the Vietnam theatre of war. They then moved north to 'Yankee' station, in the Gulf of Tonkin, about ninety miles east of Da Nang, where the 'real' war began, of anti-aircraft fire, SAMs, MiGs, and the risk of being shot down and killed or captured.

In December 1965, there was an imposing new arrival on Yankee station: the nuclear aircraft carrier *Enterprise*. She had a large and varied air wing of two F–4B Phantom squadrons, four A–4C Skyhawk squadrons, E–1B Tracers for airborne early warning, UH–2 helicopters for air-sea rescue and general ship's flight duties, and a squadron (the 'Heavy Seven') of RA–5C Vigilante bombers, converted into intelligence-gatherers, whose surveillance systems were directly linked to a new integrated operational intelligence centre (IOIC) in the ship. The IOIC gathered all the Vigilantes' information, electronic and photographic, and disseminated it to the fleet.

Enterprise flew off her first strikes against targets in North Vietnam on 17 December, and within a week had set a new record of 165 combat sorties in a day. On 22 December, *Enterprise*, *Kitty Hawk* and *Ticonderoga* attacked an industrial target in the north for the first time, when 100 aircraft made the first strike on the Uong Bi thermal power station, fifteen miles north-east of Haiphong. The plant was extensively damaged and left billowing clouds of black smoke, but two A–4s from *Enterprise* were lost to the intense flak.

By the time a Christmas truce was called on 24 December 1965, ten carriers had taken part in combat action against North Vietnam during the year and nearly 57,000 sorties had been flown. Over 100 aircraft had been lost, with 82 men killed, captured or missing; 46 had been rescued. But these naval statistics were dwarfed by those for the war as a whole.

In the air, Vietnam was a war of sheer numbers which eclipsed anything that had gone before. In Korea, in July 1953, the US Far Eastern Air Force had had 1,536 American and Allied aircraft. In Vietnam, by the middle of 1966, the Americans had 1,700 helicopters, most of them armed, 700 fixed-wing transport and reconnaissance aircraft, about 1,000 US Air Force and 400 US Navy combat aircraft, and there were 400 Vietnamese and 35 Royal Laotian Air Force aircraft. There were also 90 B–52 Stratofortress heavy bombers on Guam.

In the whole six-month siege at Dien Bien Phu, 10,400 missions were flown. By the beginning of 1966, the average *weekly* number of sorties flown by the US in Vietnam often exceeded 25,000. The 15,000 defenders of Dien Bien Phu were lucky to see 40 sorties in 24 hours. One minor incident in a remote district of Vietnam, involving 12 Americans and 300 tribesmen, had 240 sorties flown in support.

The Christmas truce lasted for thirty-seven days, while Washington waited hopefully for the communists to suggest peace talks. Instead, the North Vietnamese used the time profitably, to rebuild bombed bridges, re-lay rail tracks, repair buildings, construct extra radar, gun and SAM sites, and dig networks of tunnels as air-raid shelters and for storing petrol, ammunition and supplies.

This effort had immediate results. In January 1966, the carriers lost six aircraft and five crew, in February ten more aircraft and crew. By October, 397 aircraft had been lost, twenty-two to SAMs (which a brave and skilful pilot with exceptionally good physical co-ordination could avoid) but most to flak. By the end of the year, there were shortages in equipment and in personnel, especially Navy and Marine pilots, and the first serious rumblings of discontent about the war began in the American media.

The carriers of Yankee station had completed more than a year of intense operations. They had taken the offensive to the enemy, within the limits allowed, and had demonstrated superbly every aspect of the art of carrier warfare, except anti-submarine warfare, for which there had been no requirement.

But it had all been wasted. The ordnance had been expended, the men and the aircraft had been lost in vain. Those who had had to carry out the bombing for ROLLING THUNDER had always said that it had begun a year too late. Now, even the US high command had to admit that the offensive had failed totally to intimidate the North Vietnamese and bring them to the negotiating table.

Far from being intimidated, the North Vietnamese were continuing the war, their resourcefulness and ability to absorb punishment apparently undiminished, their morale higher than ever. In South Vietnam and in Washington, the US high command was beginning to have the first terrible suspicions that the North Vietnamese were not going to give up.

'Rolling Thunder' Dies Away

The only solution was to escalate the war, rolling the thunder ever louder and nearer Hanoi. There were still lulls, at Christmas and New Year, when Washington looked questioningly at Hanoi, hoping for some response. But, during the pauses, the North Vietnamese worked with frantic energy to repair damage and strengthen defences.

So the campaign went on, of bombing and rocketing buildings and installations, identifying and attacking SAM sites, stalking truck convoys with flares by night, strafing and bombing road and rail bridges which, being heavily defended, were the most difficult and dangerous targets of all. Although strikes were still hedged about with cautions against harming civilians, or approaching MiG airfields, or damaging third-country ships and property, the carrier air wings began to notice that the wraps were definitely coming off and political control was manifestly loosening.

In June 1966 a POL (petrol, oil, lubricants) campaign was launched under the name ROLLING THUNDER 50. For weeks Skyhawks, Intruders and Phantoms from *Franklin D. Roosevelt, Constellation, Ranger,* and *Hancock* pounded oil storage tanks and facilities from the DMZ all the way up to Haiphong. Great clouds of black smoke, rising to 35,000 feet, looked well on the newsreels. But the North Vietnamese had stored much of their stocks of oil underground. The hard truth was that ROLLING THUNDER 50 was also too late.

There was also a new opponent in the air, with the first combat appearance in March 1966 of what was to become the most famous post-war Soviet fighter, the Mach 2, delta-winged MiG–21, armed with a twin-barrel 23 mm cannon and air-to-air or air-to-surface missiles. Like its predecessors, it was highly manoeuvrable and a very dangerous opponent in turning aerial combats.

The first US Navy MiG–21 kill, on 9 October 1966, was shot down by Sidewinder missiles from an F–8 Crusader from *Oriskany*. The pilot, Commander Richard Bellinger, was forty-two years old, had flown B–17s and B–25s in the US Army in the Second World War, transferred to the Navy and flown in Korea, and was now in his third war. Bellinger had been hit by a MiG–17 and forced to eject the previous July, so this success after twenty years of flying was, as he said, 'a tremendous feeling'.

Only three weeks later, Bellinger took over *Oriskany*'s air wing after the Air Wing Commander had been killed in a serious fire on board. With thousands of gallons of high octane fuel and hundreds of tons of bombs, shells, rockets and pyrotechnics of all kinds on board, aircraft carriers were always floating fire hazards. Even when the best precautions had been taken, a pure accident could precipitate a holocaust.

On 26 October 1966, two sailors in *Oriskany* were returning unexpended parachute flares to store when one flare ignited accidentally. It was thrown in panic into a locker where it started a fire which spread to the hangar and eventually through four decks. Forty-four men were killed, among them aircrew who had just landed on after a mission and were trapped by the fire.

On 25 July 1967, *Forrestal* arrived on Yankee station to begin operations. Four days later, at 11 am on 29 July, a second launch was being readied on deck when a Zuni rocket from an F–4 on the after end of the flight deck was accidentally fired into the fuel tank of an A–4 Skyhawk, which exploded.

The explosion and the flight deck wind spread the fire to other aircraft nearby, and the whole after end of the ship was rapidly engulfed in fire. Many men were blown overboard by the explosion

or trapped in compartments below and burned to death. Destroyer escorts and, ironically, *Oriskany*, closed *Forrestal* to lend fire-fighting and medical aid, and to spray water over the burning carrier. Flight deck personnel worked with great gallantry, among exploding bombs and acres of burning petrol, to bring the main flight deck fire under control in an hour. But secondary fires below burned for another twelve hours.

One hundred and thirty-four men were killed, twenty-one aircraft were destroyed, and forty-three others damaged. *Forrestal* had to go home to Norfolk, Virginia, where the cost of repairs was estimated at $72 million.

The accident was minutely investigated, and improvements in fire-fighting techniques and equipment were introduced. But on 14 January 1969, when *Enterprise* was exercising off Hawaii before returning to Vietnam, another Zuni rocket was accidentally ignited on an F–4, starting a major fire which took three hours to bring under control. Twenty-eight men died, fifteen aircraft were destroyed, and the cost of the damage was more than $56 million. *Enterprise* could have operated her aircraft four hours later, but did not return to Yankee station until October.

In 1967 the tempo of attacks on road and rail networks in North Vietnam was stepped up, and permission was given to mine waterways, to prevent the enemy using them. In February 1967, A–6A Intruders from *Enterprise* mined the Song Ca and South Giang rivers. Attacks on MiG bases were finally allowed. On 24 April, *Kitty Hawk*'s aircraft struck a major airfield for MiG–17s and 19s at Kep, thirty-seven miles north-east of Hanoi. The MiGs rose to do battle and some furious air combats took place; US Air Force F–4s and F–105s shot down forty-six MiGs between January and June 1967.

But some restrictions remained. The port of Cam Pha, through which North Vietnam imported much of its coal, could not be attacked as long as there was a foreign ship in the harbour. Understandably, the North Vietnamese ensured there was always a foreign ship there. On 23 May 1967, a ten-mile circle, inside which bombs could not be dropped, was imposed around Hanoi. In the same month the Pentagon estimated that there were 50,000 North Vietnamese soldiers in the south, compared with 11,000 in 1965. Some 544 US combat aircraft had been lost, and 200 aircrew. The press at home were not the only ones to wonder if this was a fair exchange for the results so far achieved.

By the end of 1967, aircraft from eleven carriers had taken part in the thousands of sorties which in that year had shot down 14 MiGs in air-to-air combat, and destroyed an estimated 30 SAM sites, 187 flak batteries, 955 bridges (of which many were repaired and destroyed again and again) and literally thousands of trucks, locomotives, rail wagons, buildings and junks.

Yet, by New Year 1968, peace talks seemed as far off as ever. From 2 to 11 January, *Oriskany*, *Coral Sea* and *Ranger* carried out

Disasters at sea. Opposite above: Fire-fighting on board USS *Forrestal*, off Vietnam, 29 July, 1967. The wreckage of several F–4 Phantoms covers the after flight deck. Below: Fire on board USS *Enterprise* off Hawaii, 14 January 1969, after a rocket had accidentally ignited, setting off a train of devastating explosions

intensive strikes against bridges, SAM sites and other targets around Haiphong and Hanoi. The Tet offensive, which began in the early hours of 30 January, was another severe shock to Washington. A long and bloody siege began for Khe Sanh, an outpost near the Laotian border which the North Vietnamese and some sections of the American media called (quite wrongly, as it transpired) the 'American Dien Bien Phu'. After a seventy-one-day siege, during which the defenders were supported by Marine fixed-wing aircraft and helicopters, B–52 Stratofortresses, and 1,600 sorties by carrier aircraft, Khe Sanh was, ironically, dismantled and abandoned as having served its purpose.

In March, when the first impact of the Tet offensive had been contained, President Johnson offered to end the bombing in exchange for talks. This time, Hanoi appeared to agree, but, so as to concentrate the minds of the North Vietnamese politburo, the ROLLING THUNDER campaign continued with increased intensity between the DMZ and the 19th Parallel throughout that summer. Once he had the promise of serious talks, President Johnson halted all air attacks on the north, as from 8 am on 1 November 1968.

By that date, US Navy and Air Force pilots had flown more than 300,000 ROLLING THUNDER sorties, and dropped an estimated 860,000 tons of bombs, which was more than the tonnage dropped on Japan in the Second World War or on Korea between 1950 and 1953. They had destroyed an estimated 77 per cent of the ammunition depots in the north, 65 per cent of the POL storage, 5ε per cent of the power-generating capacity, 55 per cent of major bridges, 39 per cent of railway repair sheds, and killed about 52,000 civilians. In the process, no less than 938 US Navy and US Air Force aircraft had been lost.

But, ultimately, it was all to no avail. The North Vietnamese had never ceased to pass men and supplies down into the south throughout ROLLING THUNDER. In the north, they had had to employ some 600,000 workers in repairing buildings and constructing defences but, clearly, they could have gone on withstanding this kind of crude, bludgeoning bombing indefinitely. Paradoxically, it was the halt in the bombing, rather than the bombing itself, which had brought the North Vietnamese to the negotiating table. ROLLING THUNDER had been carried out with the utmost gallantry, skill and devotion, using the latest weaponry the world's strongest nation could provide. But, in the end, it had failed in its main purpose.

'People Sniffers' and 'Seawolves'

Flight decks make dramatic stages. The carrier aircraft on Yankee station understandably engaged much media attention. But the US Navy deployed in Vietnam a huge variety of aircraft, with widely differing roles and embodying a staggering range of technical innovations, hardly mentioned or actually still secret at the time. For example, one US Navy observation squadron, VO–67, based at Nakhom Phanom ('Naked Fanny', as the sailors called it) in Thailand, flew specially-fitted Lockheed OP–2E Neptunes to drop acoustically, seismically or organically activated sensors along the Ho Chi Minh trail. One sensor, the 'People Sniffer', contained a live bedbug, whose monitored behaviour indicated the presence of human beings.

The US Navy devoted a considerable effort to the Ho Chi Minh trail. Transport aircraft, such as AC–47s, AC–123Ks, AC–119Ks and AC–130As, were converted into 'gunships', being fitted with a sophisticated radar suite and banks of rapid-fire 7.62 mm guns, 105 mm howitzers, and 40 and 20 mm cannon to fly along the trails and blast anything that moved by day or night.

Most movement was at night, when other specially-fitted aircraft took to the air: A–6E Intruders with electro-optical sensors known as TRIM (trails, roads, interdiction multisensor), and RA–3B Skywarriors with infra-red sensors to detect the 'hot spots' of men and trucks. Some aircraft had CDIR (camouflage detection infra-red) film to reveal dead trees and vegetation laid across a

A US Navy Seawolf UH–1B helicopter and River Patrol Boat searching for Vietcong junks in the Mekong Delta

118

track to hide it. When trucks or men were detected, strikes were called down from F–4s or A–4s orbiting overhead.

Photo-reconnaissance, a vital task, was carried on from the first day of the war to the last. The US Navy used RF–8A/G Crusaders, RA–5C Vigilantes, RA–3B Skywarriors, and F–4P Phantoms. Photo-reconnaissance was unglamorous, and no way to promotion. It was also dangerous. The 'photo-bird' was normally unarmed, although sometimes escorted, and its pilot had to rely upon skill and speed to evade enemy attack. Even so, the photo-reconnaissance squadrons suffered losses out of all proportion to their numbers.

Another unglamorous role was patrolling. The patrol squadrons, flying SP–2H Neptunes, or P–3 Orions, or P–5 Marlins (the last flying boats to fly operationally in the US Navy), spent thousands of hours on OSAP (ocean surveillance patrols) and on 'Yankee station missions', which they normally flew by night, at no more than 500 feet, looking for fast-moving targets such as PT boats which might threaten the ships on Yankee station.

The patrol aircraft bore the brunt of the air effort for Operation MARKET TIME, a surveillance programme (of which OSAP and Yankee station missions were parts) by the US Navy and Vietnamese forces which maintained a continuous blockade of the entire South Vietnamese coastline, with its hundreds of miles of creeks, inlets, swamps and river estuaries, to prevent the Viet Cong supplying themselves by junks or fishing boats. The operation was carried out by Task Force 71, formed in 1965, which eventually had nearly 100 fast patrol craft and 500 armed South Vietnamese junks.

One part of MARKET TIME was GAME WARDEN. This was a 'Brown Water Navy' war on its own, in which air cushion vehicles (hovercraft), river patrol boats, specialized shallow-draught vessels and helicopters carried out an extended patrol of the rivers and waterways in the Mekong delta and the Rung Sat – the swampy areas lying between Saigon and the sea – stopping river traffic to search for Viet Cong and their supplies. Here the US Navy used 'Hueys', UH–1B Iroquois helicopters, to carry sea-air landing (SEAL) assault platoons. Huey gunships armed with machine-guns and rocket tubes, known as 'Seawolves', provided fire support and reconnaissance for river patrol craft.

The helicopter was ubiquitous in Vietnam. The abiding image of that war in the public's mind is very probably a helicopter gunship. But much use was made, both by the US Navy and the Marines, of the giant twin-rotor Boeing CH–46 Sea Knight for carrying men and stores ashore or across country. At the peak of operations, an average of 770,000 tons of supplies per month were landed from US ships.

Troops were often flown ashore by helicopter. HMAS *Sydney*, no longer classed as a carrier, was recommissioned from reserve as a troop and equipment transport. Known as the 'Vung Tau Ferry', she made twenty trips to Vietnam, anchoring off the coast while the troops were ferried to shore in RAAF CH–47C Chinooks.

Task Force 77 at sea always needed replacement parts, relief personnel, supplies of all kinds, and mail which were flown out from Cubi Point in the Philippines in Grumman C–1 Traders or C–2 Greyhounds, cargo versions of the S–2 Tracker ASW (anti-submarine warfare) aircraft and the E–2 Hawkeye, by the Pacific Fleet tactical support squadron. Theirs was certainly an unsung role. But one image at least from Vietnam is therefore reassuringly domestic – of a Trader or a Greyhound labouring out to find the carriers on Yankee station, to deliver 1,600 lbs of their mail.

A Chinook helicopter lifting a Pilatus Porter aircraft from the deck of HMAS *Sydney* off Vietnam, December 1969

From 'Linebacker' to the End

By the end of 1968, there were 540,000 US troops in Vietnam. Richard Nixon was President and was anxious to bring the war to a conclusion but not to go down in history as the first American President to lose. Since 1967, the majority of the American people had felt that it had been wrong to get involved in Vietnam, 'but now that we're there, let's win – or get out'. But in 1968 there had been huge anti-war demonstrations in Washington DC and other major American cities. Richard Nixon's only realistic course of action was large-scale withdrawal from Vietnam.

Meanwhile, Task Force 77 aircraft still flew over South Vietnam, mainly in the 1 Corps area, south of the DMZ, where they flew 1,025 sorties in one month, July 1969, alone. By now, some carriers had been to Vietnam several times. In November 1970, *Bon Homme Richard* went home to the United States after her sixth deployment to Vietnam, leaving only two of the smaller *Essex* '27C' programme carriers, *Hancock* and *Oriskany*, still in commission.

Oriskany had two squadrons of Vought A–7 Corsair IIs, which had first arrived on Yankee station in *Ranger* in December 1967. Looking very similar to the F–8 Crusader, but actually a new and quite different aircraft, the A–7 Corsair II was intended to replace the A–4 Skyhawk as the US Navy's light strike aircraft. In fact, A–7s and A–4s operated together for the rest of the Vietnam war, the larger carriers, such as *America*, having the latest A–7E Corsairs and the 27C carriers having the A–4F.

It was *Hancock*'s A–4Fs which supported the South Vietnamese incursion into Laos in February 1971, code-named LAM SON 719, after a Vietnamese victory over the Chinese in the fifteenth century. The twentieth-century venture was not so successful and South Vietnamese troops had withdrawn from Laos by the end of March. Saigon claimed a victory, but traffic was moving again along the Ho Chi Minh trail and there were targets for the A–4 'truck-busters' in a very short time.

The carriers offshore were now operating in a kind of limbo, neither at war nor at peace. Although the flying was just as dangerous and lives were still liable to be lost, and the aircrew flew with as much skill and dedication as before, the war seemed to have lost what little sense of purpose and direction it had ever had.

'The frustration comes on all levels,' an A–4 pilot in *Hancock* wrote in his diary. 'We fly a limited aircraft, drop limited ordnance, on rare targets in a severely limited amount of time. Worst of all, we do all this in a limited and highly unpopular war . . . We're in, have time for two runs and we're bingo for either time or fuel . . . One of the ways to slice through the webbing and be free, at least for the moment, of almost all frustration is to press the attack home and while you jink and claw away from all the reaching AAA hear the FAC [Forward Air Controller] – "Shit hot, two, you got the son of a bitch!"'

Early in 1972, the North Vietnamese began to bring more and more mobile SAM sites south, closer to the DMZ. The two carriers on Yankee station, *Coral Sea* and *Constellation* (both on their sixth Vietnam cruise), joined in February by *Hancock*, responded with increased protective-reaction raids against them.

On 19 January, one of *Constellation*'s F–4Js of VF–96, a crack flying unit which had twice won the Clifton Trophy for the Navy's outstanding fighter squadron, shot down a MiG–21 – the 112th MiG kill of the war and the Navy's tenth. The pilot, Lieutenant Randall H. Cunningham and his Radar Intercept Officer Lieutenant Willie Driscoll, became the Navy's first and only Vietnam fighter 'aces' (with five kills) and the first 'team aces' in aerial warfare.

Anti-SAM strikes had been a major part of the USAF and US Navy's electronic counter-measures (ECM) campaign since the early days of the war. Latterly, almost every strike, whatever its purpose, was accompanied by an ECM escort, often F–4 Phantoms, specially fitted with radar-suppression and jamming pods.

Most of the US Navy's anti-SAM IRON HAND strikes were flown by A–4 Skyhawks. When a SAM approached, warning lights glowed on the A–4 cockpit panels and pilots could hear in their headphones a warning 'warble', known as the 'Samsong', after the 'Fansong' ground radar which controlled the SAMs. The A–4s

USS *New Orleans*, the amphibious assault ship in Force 78 which cleared mines from Vietnamese waters in 1973, at anchor in Subic Bay in the Philippines

were armed with AGM–45A Shrike missiles which literally 'rode' down the beam of the Fansong radars. (After a time, the North Vietnamese countered by switching their radars on and off, to give the homing missiles less signal time.)

In the early days, the main ECM aircraft was the ageing EF–10B Skyknight. This was superseded by the EA–6A, a modified Intruder equipped with tactical ECM equipment. But in 1972, the first EA–6B Prowlers arrived in *America* and *Enterprise*. They were lengthened versions of the Intruder, with three or four crew and an extensive ECM kit capable of jamming SAM radar, interception radar, and radio transmissions.

The Prowlers had a very busy introduction to Vietnam, with the steadily increasing enemy activity which followed the North Vietnamese invasion of 30 March 1972, the Thursday before Good Friday, when three North Vietnamese divisions crossed the DMZ. They were the first of an eventual twelve combat divisions, with 120,000 troops and using tanks in force for the first time in the war, which invaded South Vietnam over that Easter weekend.

President Nixon responded more vigorously than any of his predecessors. B–52s unloaded hundreds of tons of bombs on North Vietnam and went on in April to bomb Haiphong and Hanoi itself, which had become the most heavily defended city in air warfare history, with fifteen SAM sites, over 600 anti-aircraft guns of various calibres and several MiG–17 and MiG–21 airfields nearby.

In April and May, carrier strength built up to five ships, *Saratoga*, *Hancock*, *Midway*, *Constellation*, and *Kitty Hawk*, which ranged the entire length of Vietnam, their air wings striking at Quang Tri in the south one day and at Haiphong the next. In May, A–6 Corsairs from three carriers mined the harbours of Haiphong, Hon Gai, and Cam Pha in the north, and Thanh Hoa, Vinh, Quang Khe and Dong Hoi in the south. 'What happened,' said Vice Admiral William P. Mack, Commander Seventh Fleet, 'was that all traffic into Vietnam, except across the Chinese border, stopped. Within ten days there was not a missile or a shell being fired at us from the beach. The North Vietnamese ran out of ammunition, just as we always said they would.'

The American aerial offensive of 1972, code-named LINEBACKER, was of a quite unprecedented ferocity and accuracy. It began with raids mounted from Thailand and continued from May with LINEBACKER II raids from Guam. The attacks, which went on until December, were this time more like rapiers than bludgeons. In May 1972, F–4 Phantoms with laser-guided 'smart' bombs finally destroyed the Thanh Hoa bridge, eighty miles south of Hanoi, which had had more than 700 sorties flown against it over the years and had resisted many sorts of weapon including, in March 1967, US Navy 'Walleye' TV-guided missiles.

In July, Task Force 77 supported LINEBACKER with six carriers, *America*, *Hancock*, *Kitty Hawk*, *Midway*, *Saratoga* and *Oriskany* (on her seventh Vietnam combat deployment), patrolling the whole coastline of Vietnam, striking at North Vietnamese troops in the south, at radar and SAM sites in the north, and flying frequent sorties over the Ho Chi Minh trail. The electronic EA–6As and EA–6B Prowlers were particularly busy, making three or even four sorties a day to cover the ongoing bomber raids.

Nearly 3,500 sorties were flown during LINEBACKER by B–52s, tactical strike aircraft, and other support aircraft. Nearly 1,000 SAMs were fired at attacking aircraft. Fifteen B–52s were shot down. But it did seem that, for once, all the effort had been worthwhile, although as always in Vietnam appearances were to prove deceptive. Peace talks were set to resume on 8 January 1973. An F–4 Phantom from *Midway* shot down a MiG–17 over the Gulf of Tonkin on 9 January. Thus fighters from *Midway* shot down the first and the last MiGs of the war.

A ceasefire agreement was signed on 23 January 1973. In February, a US minesweeping force including helicopters began to sweep up the mines so recently laid in Vietnamese harbours. On 12 February, the first POWs to be released from Vietnam arrived in the Philippines; 566 were returned, leaving many unaccounted for.

The US Navy shot down fifty-nine MiGs in air-to-air combat, two AN–2 biplane transports, one probable MiG with a Talos SAM, and several other probables. The USAF shot down 137 MiGs, including two by B–52 gunners. Experience had shown the disadvantages of the F–4 Phantom's all-missile armament. Missiles were certainly preferable at a distance or at night. But in close combat, especially against a quick-turning MiG, most pilots also wanted an internally-mounted gun.

However, American air losses in Vietnam gave both the US Navy and the USAF food for thought. Over 3,700 American aircraft of all types had been lost in action. Two thousand American airmen had been lost, with nearly 1,400 missing in action. A total of 7.4 million tons of bombs had been dropped on Indo-China since 1965 (compared with 2 million tons of bombs dropped by the US in all theatres during the Second World War).

There remained one last duty for the carriers to perform off Vietnam. No matter what had been lost or won on the battlefield, no matter what had been agreed or disagreed at the negotiating table, the North Vietnamese politburo never wavered from its main purpose, which was the conquest of the whole of Vietnam.

By 1975, the Ho Chi Minh trail was no longer a collection of jungle paths, but a metalled highway with lay-bys, parking spaces and fixed AA gun emplacements. In its way it symbolized the passage of events for the North Vietnamese. Down this road men and supplies had continued to pour. In the early months of 1975, there was a rapid and disastrous collapse of morale amongst the South Vietnamese administration and army. Positions which had been defended for years crumbled overnight.

With 120,000 troops converging upon Saigon, the North Vietnamese were ready to inflict the final, mortal blow, the 'Ho Chi

Minh Campaign', which they began on 7 April with the shelling of Saigon itself. Washington and the President (now Gerald Ford, Nixon having resigned over Watergate the previous August) washed their hands of Indo-China, although Operation BABYLIFT was organized, by which 3,000 orphans, mostly of mixed blood, were airlifted out of Saigon.

On 12 April, Operation EAGLE PULL, the evacuation of the American embassy, was carried out by Marine helicopters of HMH–462 and 463. On 27 April, the North Vietnamese brought Saigon's last air base, Tan Son Nhut, under long-range artillery fire. USAF C–130s and C–141s shuttled back and forth from Guam, where refugee camps were opened.

Offshore, *Midway* and *Enterprise* (with the new fighter aircraft, the F–14A Tomcat) covered events. At noon on 29 April, A–7 Corsairs, A–6 Intruders and F–14A Tomcats swept over Saigon as Operation FREQUENT WIND, the final evacuation, began. The remaining 1,500 Americans in the city went to pre-arranged Saigon rooftops whence sixty CH–53 helicopters lifted them out to ships of the Seventh Fleet.

But the evacuation soon became a panic. US Marines on the

Embassy rooftop used rifle butts and, latterly, tear gas to beat off a terrified mob of South Vietnamese, all fighting to be saved. Almost all promises to save loyal South Vietnamese officials, embassy staff, police, CIA informers and Viet Cong deserters went by the board. The CIA even left its records behind.

The helicopter airlift went on until the early hours of 30 April, when over 8,000 people had been evacuated. In this 'Night of the Helicopters', the big Sea Stallions made more than forty sorties, taking 2,000 people back to *Midway*. In the contemptuous words of the North Vietnamese army commander, General Van Tien Dung, 'after 30 years of military intervention and adventures in Vietnam . . . the US ambassador had to crawl onto the roof of the embassy building to escape'. At 1100 a North Vietnamese tank smashed through the gates of the presidential palace in Saigon.

Of the 2,300,000 Americans who served in Vietnam, 46,370 servicemen died in battle between 1961 and 1974, with another 300,000 wounded. The ARVN suffered some 184,000 soldiers killed between 1961 and the January 1973 ceasefire. The North Vietnamese Army and the Viet Cong probably suffered casualties of about 900,000 between 1961 and 1974.

Farewell to HMS *Albion* from Wessex helicopters of 845 Squadron as the ship arrived in Portsmouth to pay off for the last time, 25 November 1972

Into the Seventies

AS the decade of the 1970s opened, a number of navies had their own air arms, with at least one aircraft carrier. Almost all the carriers were ex-British. Argentina had two: *Independencia* (HMS *Warrior*) and *25 de Mayo* (HMS *Venerable*, and until 1968 the Dutch *Karel Doorman*). Australia had *Melbourne* (HMS *Majestic*) and *Sydney* (HMS *Terrible*), Brazil *Minas Gerais* (HMS *Vengeance*), and Canada *Bonaventure* (HMS *Powerful*). France still had *Arromanches* (*Colossus*), but also built two 32,000 ton, 30-aircraft, 32 knot carriers, *Clemenceau* and *Foch*, completed in 1961 and 1963 respectively. The French Navy also had *Jeanne D'Arc*, a peacetime training ship, which could be modified to a helicopter carrier in time of war. Only the Spanish Navy went American, with their *Dedalo* (USS *Wilmington*).

One ex-British light fleet carrier, HMS *Hercules*, saw action as the Indian Navy's *Vikrant* in the fourteen-day war between India and Pakistan in December 1971. She was equipped with eighteen Sea Hawks of No. 300 Squadron ('The White Tigers') which had formed and worked up at RNAS Brawdy, in Pembrokeshire, in July 1960, and four French Breguet Alize turbo-prop anti-submarine aircraft. Operating in the Bay of Bengal, INS *Vikrant*'s Sea Hawks bombed and rocketed airfields and shipping at Cox's Bazaar and Chittagong, in East Pakistan. The Alizes carried out night mine-laying raids on shipping channels and harbours. The Pakistan Navy had no carrier and *Vikrant* had complete command of the air at sea, as the Indian Air Force also had, after about the fifth day of fighting, on land.

Having supplied many of the world's navies with aircraft carriers, the Royal Navy – or rather, British politicians – then began to turn away from fixed-wing carrier flying. A new 55,000 ton carrier, known then (and ever since) as CVA01, had been announced officially on 30 July 1963, but cancelled by the incoming Labour Defence Minister, Denis Healey, on 22 February 1966.

This seemed to be the signal for a period of decline. *Victorious* recommissioned during refit in August 1967, but then had to be scrapped after a disastrous fire on board in November. *Centaur* was taken out of service in 1966, *Eagle* in 1972, and both were then scrapped. By 1973, *Hermes* had been converted to a Commando carrier, with no capacity to operate fixed-wing aircraft. *Bulwark* also remained in the Commando carrier role, but *Albion* was sent for scrapping in 1973. The cruisers *Blake* and *Tiger* were converted into command helicopter cruisers, but, like all hybrids, they were both ugly and unsuccessful.

The Royal Navy's only fixed-wing carrier was *Ark Royal*, which recommissioned after a major refit in February 1970. With her F–4 Phantoms (purchased from America) of 892 Squadron, Buccaneer Mk 2s of 809 Squadron, AEW Gannets of 849 Squadron, and Sea King anti-submarine helicopters of 824, *Ark Royal* was the most powerful strike carrier the Fleet Air Arm had ever possessed. She enjoyed a busy and much-publicized existence until she paid off for the last time in December 1978.

129

After *Ark Royal*, the Royal Navy faced a future in which it would no longer have its own organic air power, when maritime air power would be provided by land-based RAF aircraft, all fixed-wing recruiting and training would cease, and the Fleet Air Arm would become an all-helicopter service, with the Sea King as its main battle aircraft. Fleet Air Arm pilots of fixed-wing aircraft could either transfer to the RAF, convert to helicopter flying, or leave.

Meanwhile the US Navy, despite persistent sniping, principally from submariners, that the carrier made 'too big and juicy a target' and was 'putting all your eggs in one vulnerable basket', continued to build and commission big carriers. By the end of the decade, the US Navy had two more giant 82,000 ton, 90-aircraft, nuclear-powered carriers, *Nimitz* and *Dwight D. Eisenhower*, to join *Enterprise*, and a third of the same class, *Carl Vinson*, building. These were awe-inspiring ships, with complements of nearly 6,500 men, including the air wings. They had two nuclear reactors, compared with *Enterprise*'s eight, which could steam for thirteen years, or an estimated one million miles, between refuellings.

The US Navy also had four large carriers of the *Kitty Hawk* and *John F. Kennedy* classes, four *Forrestals*, and *Coral Sea* and *Midway*, with five remaining carriers of the *Intrepid* and *Hancock* classes, two modernized *Essex* class, and fourteen helicopter-carrying amphibious warfare carriers of the *Blue Ridge*, *Tarawa* and *Iwo Jima* classes. Furthermore, in 1978, the US Navy began upon a carrier service life extension programme (SLEP), designed to extend the lives of the larger carriers well into the twenty-first century.

US naval aviation at that time had some 7,000 aircraft, including thirteen carrier air wings and twenty-four maritime reconnaissance/patrol squadrons, using F–4 Phantom and F–14 Tomcat fighters, A–6 Intruder and A–7 Corsair attack aircraft, RA–5C Vigilante and RF–8G Crusader reconnaissance aircraft, E–2 Hawkeyes for airborne early warning, EA–6B Prowlers for electronic warfare, S–3 Vikings for anti-submarine, and P–3 Orions for maritime patrols. The Navy also used SH–3 Sea Kings and SH–2 LAMPS (light airborne multi-purpose system) helicopters for anti-submarine work, RH–53 Sea Stallions for mine counter-measures, and UH–46 Sea Knights for helicopter support. There were also US Marine fighter, attack and reconnaissance squadrons, as well as Marine squadrons with AH–1 Sea Cobra helicopter gunships, and transport squadrons using UH–1 Iroquois (Hueys), Sea Stallions and Sea Knights.

By comparison with this array of naval air power, the Soviet Navy's air arm appeared insignificant. But it grew, beginning with the appearance in the late 1960s of the two 19,000 ton *protivo lodochny kreysers* (anti-submarine cruisers) *Moskva* and *Leningrad*, each carrying eighteen Hormone ASW helicopters. But in the early 1970s there were reports of a much bigger Soviet anti-submarine cruiser. This was the 42,000 ton *Kiev*, commissioned in

HMS *Ark Royal*, June 1977, with Phantom FG.1s of 892 Squadron, Gannet AEW3s of B flight, 849 Squadron, Buccaneer S.2s of 809 Squadron, and Wessex Mk 1 of ship's Search and Rescue flight on deck

1976, and followed by two more of the same class, *Minsk* and *Komsomolec*. They carried thirty to thirty-five aircraft, with a usual 'mix' of eighteen Hormone helicopters and twelve Yak–36 'Forger' vertical/short take-off and landing (V/STOL) aircraft, and a considerable missile armament.

It seemed ironic that just as the Royal Navy was retiring from the main field of naval aviation, the Soviet Navy should emerge with ships which were large aircraft carriers in everything but name capable of projecting Soviet naval air power worldwide.

Left: Two A–7 Corsair IIs being launched from the 95,000-ton nuclear powered USS *Nimitz* with A–6 Intruders and an F–14 Tomcat in the deck park, June 1978

Above: Russian air power at sea. A Yak–36 'Forger' VTOL aircraft hovering over the 42,000-ton Soviet aircraft carrier *Kiev*, and (below) the flight deck of *Kiev*

Flying Bedsteads and Ski Jumps

THE cancellation of CVA01 in 1966 proved to be a blessing in disguise for the Royal Navy, although it was a blessing well disguised at the time. The prospect of a future without carriers, when the last of the existing hulls went to scrap, concentrated minds wonderfully to seek some other solution.

As the fixed-wing element of the Fleet Air Arm began inevitably to wither away (although *Ark Royal*'s life was extended to the end of 1978), the best hope for the future clearly lay in the helicopter. Frigates and above carried at least one helicopter – from 1964, the Westland Wasp which, from 1976, began to be replaced by the Westland Lynx – for anti-submarine warfare and ship's flight duties. The Westland Sea King, an excellent design which was first delivered to the Navy late in 1969, emerged as the Royal Navy's major front-line aircraft.

The Sea King weighed as much as 21,000 lbs at full load, but it was more than just a large helicopter: it was a fully-integrated, all-weather, hunter-killer anti-submarine weapons system, with radar, sonar, computerized automatic flight control, a crew of four (two pilots, observer and sonar operator), a speed of about 130 mph and a range of nearly 800 miles, and it was armed with homing torpedoes or depth-charges.

Such a weapons system needed a suitable fighting platform. The US Navy had commissioned the amphibious assault ship *Iwo Jima*, the first ship in the world to be designed and constructed specifically to operate helicopters, as long ago as August 1961. But *Iwo Jima* looked very like an aircraft carrier, a term suddenly unfashionable in Whitehall.

Over the years, the concept slowly emerged of a *cruiser*, with enough flat surface on her upper deck to operate several Sea Kings in the anti-submarine role. So, it was to be what was called a *through-deck* cruiser. She was to be a *command* cruiser as well, able to exercise command and control of naval and maritime air forces. She was also to contribute to area air defence, with missiles.

The new ship, to be called *Invincible*, was emphatically *not* a carrier. She was to be a through-deck command *cruiser*. As such, she survived a sustained campaign of committee battles, escaped a thousand paper ambushes, and ran successive gauntlets of Treasury hawks and back-stabbing lobbyists for the RAF who had never troubled to conceal their delight at the death of fixed-wing naval flying.

Invincible was ordered in April 1973, laid down in July, launched by HM the Queen in May 1977, and accepted into the Navy in March 1980. As the years went by, nobody had ever dared to point out that the 'see-through cruiser', as she was ironically called, was looking more and more like an aircraft carrier. She was still officially a cruiser, with fourteen aircraft and twin Sea Dart surface-to-air missile launchers. At 16,000 tons and 678 feet long, with a crew of nearly 1,000 officers and men, she was the biggest new warship the Navy had had for more than twenty-five years.

HMS *Invincible* at speed

Nine Sea King helicopters of
826 Squadron in formation over
Cornwall, 1977

Scarcely believing their luck, the Royal Navy had emerged with an aircraft carrier and, *mirabile dictu*, the prospect of two more, *Illustrious* and *Indomitable* (to be renamed *Ark Royal*).

The Navy might have been well satisfied with a new class of helicopter carriers. But there was more to come, due to the fortunate arrival of a new concept of aircraft design which had begun with Rolls Royce's appropriately named 'Flying Bedstead' in 1953. The idea was easy to grasp, but very difficult to achieve: an aircraft which could take off vertically and then, by altering the angle of engine thrust, fly forwards in normal flight.

Hawker Siddeley developed such an aircraft, to demonstrate the technology, in the P.1127 prototype which first flew on 19 November 1960, and carried out deck landing trials on board *Ark Royal* in February 1963.

The Kestrel, as it was later called, aroused more interest in America, and especially in the US Marine Corps, than in the United Kingdom. Trials were carried out in the US carrier *Independence* and the amphibious transport dock *Raleigh* in 1966, and a year later on the helicopter landing deck of the Italian cruiser *Andrea Doria*. In 1969 there were more deck trials on another US amphibious transport dock, *La Salle*.

From the Kestrel evolved the VTOL (vertical take-off and landing) Harrier GR Mk 1, which first flew on 28 December 1967 and entered RAF service with No. 1 Squadron in 1969. A Harrier carried out trials on the helicopter deck of the cruiser *Blake* in 1969. In May 1971, RAF Harriers of No. 1 Squadron embarked for trials in *Ark Royal* in the Moray Firth, their pilots having had deck-landing training on a painted 'flight deck' at their base at RAF Wittering, near Peterborough.

In 1972, a two-seater Harrier flew twenty-two sorties in two days from INS *Vikrant* in the Indian Ocean. Harriers also landed on the wooden deck of the Spanish *Dedalo*; the Spaniards later bought eight AV–8As, or Matadors as they called them, from America.

The US version, the McDonnell Douglas AV–8A Harrier, was first delivered to the US Marine Corps in January 1971, and underwent trials in the amphibious assault ship *Guadalcanal* and the transport dock *Coronado* the same year. AV–8As embarked for two longer periods in the amphibious assault ship *Guam*, off the east coast of the US in 1972 and in the North Atlantic in 1973, flying 300 sorties, some in weather too rough for helicopter flying. In September 1976, fourteen AV–8As of Marine squadron VMA–231 embarked in the carrier *Franklin D. Roosevelt* with the Sixth Fleet in the Mediterranean. In eight months on board, they flew over 2,000 sorties, twenty per cent of them at night.

By 1978, the Harrier had flown from some thirty ships of nine navies around the world, but was still not in service with the Royal Navy. Approval was given in May 1975 to convert the Harrier GR Mk 1 into the Sea Harrier, with a raised cockpit, a redesigned nose assembly to accommodate an improved avionics suite, including

The Hawker P. 1127 making the first-ever vertical landing by a jet aircraft on a carrier at sea (HMS *Ark Royal*, February 1963)

Blue Fox radar, an improved Rolls Royce Pegasus 104 engine, an auto-pilot, a new nav-attack system, new weapon installations, and the removal of magnesium from exposed portions of the airframe.

The first Harrier with RN markings did trials in *Hermes* in February 1977. The true Sea Harrier made its maiden flight on 20 August 1978, its first deck landing on *Hermes* on 14 November, and was delivered to the Navy on 18 June 1979. It was a single-seat V/STOL fighter, reconnaissance and strike aircraft, with a top speed of 740 mph, and a loaded weight of 25,000 lbs. The armament was two fixed 30 mm Aden cannons, two Sidewinder missiles, or two Martel or Harpoon air-to-surface missiles, or five 1,000 lb bombs. The first front-line Sea Harrier squadron, 800 Squadron, commissioned in April 1980.

The Sea Harrier's operational effectiveness was dramatically increased by a device which was first put forward in 1973 by Lieutenant Commander D. R. Taylor RN and nicknamed by his

wife Iris the 'ski jump'. It earned its inventor an award of £25,000 and, like the angled deck, was basically so simple an idea everybody else kicked themselves for missing it.

The 'ski jump' was essentially an upward curving runway which imparted a semi-ballistic trajectory to the aircraft at take-off. The 'ski jump' increased the Sea Harrier's effective take-off speed by some 30 knots, added some 2,000 lbs to the payload, and cut its reaction time to two minutes from starting the engine to fully airborne. Furthermore, the carrier did not need to turn into the wind for launching, and could carry on launching in sea states which would otherwise have been unsafe. This resulted in large savings in time and fuel consumption for both ship and aircraft.

After all her trials, *Invincible* entered service with a 'ski jump' of 7 degrees, and an aircraft complement of five V/STOL Sea Harriers and nine Sea King helicopters. Against all the odds, the Fleet Air Arm had survived into the 1980s with a new aircraft carrier and a new fixed-wing high performance aircraft.

The Falklands

Previous pages: HMS *Hermes* en route to the Falklands, April 1982
Right: Crowds waving farewell to HMS *Invincible* sailing from Portsmouth on her way to the Falklands

'I SUPPOSE the Spanish Armada enjoyed a send-off like this!' said one of *Hermes*' Sea King pilots, with a certain amount of foreboding. It was the morning of Monday 5 April 1982 and *Hermes* was at sea, heading for the South Atlantic, having just played her part in an amazing scene which few in England had ever expected to see in their lifetimes. Every road, jetty, building and vantage point in Portsmouth and Gosport had been black with people, bands had played, flags and banners waved, to bid farewell and God speed to the largest fleet to sail from the shores of England since the Second World War.

Nobody was more surprised by the rapid assembly and dispatch of the British task force than the Argentinians. The behaviour of successive British governments had seemed to indicate that the United Kingdom did not greatly care about the fate of the Falkland Islands which, for many years, the Argentinians had believed, rightly or wrongly, belonged to Argentina. Thus, when the Argentinians invaded the Falkland Islands, they might well have done so in the genuine belief that they were giving an actual if somewhat premature military reality to what had always been a political probability.

The pretext for the invasion was the landing of some Argentinian scrap metal workers on South Georgia in March. To give military support to the contingent on South Georgia, which was 700 miles east of the Falklands and 1,100 miles from Argentina, it was necessary also to invade the Falklands.

The majority of the ships for Operation ROSARIO, the Argentine invasion of the Falklands, had sailed on 28 March, with the carrier *25 de Mayo*, a tanker and escorting destroyers, forming Task Force 20, the support and covering force. A battalion of Marines, embarked in an LST and bound for Port Stanley, were in the amphibious task force, TF 40, escorted by destroyers, corvettes and the submarine *Santa Fe*. Task Force 60, of one corvette and a supply ship, went to South Georgia.

The invasion force arrived off the islands after nightfall on 1 April and the first landings began at 9.15 pm. After a spirited resistance by the tiny Royal Marine garrison, the islands were surrendered on 2 April. The first Argentine Air Force C–130 Hercules landed on Port Stanley airfield at 8.30 am. South Georgia surrendered on 3 April.

Only two days later, Task Group 317.8, known ineradicably to the British public as the 'Task Force', was steaming south, to begin the recapture of the Falklands, code-named Operation CORPORATE. The impression given in the media was that the Task Force was a large fleet of ships which headed steadily and inexorably south. In fact, TG 317.8 began with only six ships, with other ships joining and leaving during the passage south. More than once ships stopped, turned round and retraced their tracks because of political or other considerations.

The first ships to sail were *Hermes* and *Invincible*, the frigates *Alacrity* and *Antelope*, the Royal Fleet Auxiliary (RFA) tanker

Super Etendard of the 3rd
Escuadra, Aviación Naval
Argentina

Olmeda from Portsmouth, and the RFA replenishment ship
Resource from Plymouth. The heart of the force was the two
carriers. Because of NATO commitments, *Hermes* had had
her anti-submarine warfare capability restored in the 1970s,
while retaining her Commando role. She had the most up-to
date communications outfit and was to become the flagship.
She sailed with eleven Sea Harriers of 800 and 899 Squadrons
and eighteen Sea Kings of 826 and part of 846 Commando squadrons. *Invincible* had eight Sea Harriers of 801 and nine Sea
Kings of 820.

Altogether, six ships sailed with nineteen Sea Harriers and
forty-five helicopters of five basic types flown by six naval and
Commando brigade squadrons. But those nineteen Sea Harriers
seemed a very meagre allowance of fighters to give air cover to the
ships and to an amphibious landing, if there should be one, over a
supply line of 8,000 miles.

Shortly after leaving Portsmouth, *Invincible*'s engineers heard a
sound 'they recognized and didn't like' from the starboard shaft
gear coupling. A new coupling, weighing $2\frac{1}{2}$ tons, was flown on
board by Chinook helicopter. Repairs were completed at sea by the
time the ship arrived at Ascension Island on 15 April.

Several destroyers and frigates had already arrived at Ascension, most of them having been diverted from a NATO exercise in the Mediterranean. They included *Glamorgan*, flying the flag of Rear Admiral J.F. ('Sandy') Woodward, Flag Officer First Flotilla and now Commander Task Group 317.8, *Antrim*, *Yarmouth*, *Broadsword*, *Brilliant*, *Arrow*, *Alacrity*, *Coventry*, *Glasgow*, and *Plymouth*, and the RFAs *Fort Austin*, *Resource*, *Olmeda*, and *Tidespring*.

From Wideawake to South Georgia

It seemed that the Argentinians had entirely overlooked Ascension Island in the South Atlantic, 3,700 nautical miles from the United Kingdom, and 3,300 from the Falkland Islands. Certainly, they grossly underestimated the value of this outcrop of volcanic rock, seven miles wide and thirty-four square, with a 10,000-foot-long runway at Wideawake, as a halfway staging post, anchorage, refuelling depot and transit camp.

At Ascension, ships 'cross-decked' into their right place and right order troops, stores and equipment which had been loaded in haste in the United Kingdom. Vertical replenishments (VERTREPS) by helicopter took place by day and by night. There was live firing practice with every size and sort of weapon, from rifles to missiles, and exercises in embarkation and amphibious landings.

Air traffic at Wideawake soared from the usual one or two USAF aircraft a week to 500 aircraft movements a day by 16 April, making it temporarily the busiest airfield in the world. Eventually, seventeen Victors, three Vulcans, four Hercules, four Nimrods for long-range maritime reconnaissance, four Phantoms for local air defence and four support helicopters were based there. The number of extra UK personnel on the island rose from nil to over 800 in three weeks, and to a peak of over 1,400, mostly in temporary accommodation.

When Admiral Sir John Fieldhouse, C-in-C Fleet (and now also Commander Task Force 317) flew in from London on 17 April, on the staff conference agenda were the estimates (much of which had come from *Jane's Fighting Ships*) of Argentinian naval strength and air power. Besides the aircraft carrier, they had one ex-US cruiser, four submarines, two British-built Type 42 destroyers, and a number of other destroyers and frigates, to a total of some seventy-three warships.

One first estimate of Argentinian air strength was 247 fighter and attack aircraft. In fact, the Fuerza Aerea Argentina had eighteen A–4C and thirty-six ex-US Navy A–4B Skyhawks, thirty-seven Daggers (Israeli-built versions of the Mirage 5) and seventeen Mirage IIIs operational. Embarked in *25 de Mayo* were eight of the Navy's ten A–4Q Skyhawks, four of the five S–2E Trackers, three out of their seven A1–03 Alouette helicopters, and five H–3

Argentinian aircraft. Right:
1A–58A Pucará at Port Stanley.
Centre: Douglas A–4Q Skyhawk
aboard the Argentinian carrier
25 de Mayo. Bottom:
Argentinian Dagger

ASW Sea Kings. Ashore were ten Navy MB–339 Aeromacchis, and five SUE Super Etendards, of which four were serviceable.

Not counting three Air Force squadrons of IA–58 Pucarás, this was a total of 142 fighter and attack aircraft –very much lower than initial estimates, but still outnumbering the Task Force's fighters by six to one. When Task Group 317.8 sailed south from Ascension on 17 April, with Admiral Woodward flying his flag in *Hermes*, it was already clear that they would have to grind down the Argentinian air forces by attrition, or else flout one of the basic lessons of the Second World War: no opposed amphibious landing should be attempted without local air superiority.

On 11 April a special task group TG 317.9, of the destroyer *Antrim*, the frigate *Plymouth*, and the RFA tanker *Tidespring* (with two Wessex Mk 5s of C Flight 845 Squadron and M Company of 42 Commando RM embarked) was formed to carry out Operation PARAQUAT, the reoccupation of South Georgia, with Captain B.A. Young, CO of *Antrim*, as Commander Task Group 317.9.

The task group was joined on 14 April by the survey vessel HMS *Endurance*. It was rumours in 1981 of *Endurance*'s possible withdrawal from the Antarctic which had helped to convince the Argentinians that HM Government was no longer interested in the Falklands; she had spent an anxious time since the invasion trying to make her plum-coloured hull as unobtrusive as possible among the icebergs. Her ship's company were surprised and delighted to be cheered by the other ships.

On arrival off South Georgia on 21 April, the ships' first task was to 'insert' surveillance parties of the Special Boat Squadron and the SAS, who were landed on the Fortuna Glacier by the two Wessex 5s and *Antrim*'s own Wessex 3. The weather deteriorated overnight, with storm force winds of 70 mph, and the SAS had to be taken off. All three Wessex landed with great difficulty on the glacier but one Wessex 5 crashed in 'white-out' conditions whilst taking off. The survivors were taken on board the other two Wessex, but the second Wessex 5 also crashed.

In a superbly sustained feat of airmanship, *Antrim*'s Wessex 3 pilot, Lieutenant Commander Ian Stanley, took his passengers back to the ship and then, after two attempts and during a lucky break in the appalling weather, returned to the glacier. Again, he succeeded in landing, recovered the survivors of the other two Wessex, and took them all back to the ship.

By 24 April, when the Type 22 frigate *Brilliant* joined the operation, there had been reports of an Argentinian submarine in the area. Early on the 25th, *Antrim*'s Wessex 3 was searching off Cumberland Bay when one sweep of her radar picked up a tiny echo. Closing his target, Stanley identified it as an Argentinian submarine, and attacked.

'What a moment!' wrote Lieutenant Chris Parry, Stanley's observer. 'Every observer's dream – to have a real live submarine caught in the trap with two depth-charges ready to go! As Ian called "On top now . . . now . . . now!" I saw the fin of a submarine pass under the aircraft through the gap around the sonar housing and I released both depth-charges.'

The charges exploded close to the port side of the submarine (actually *Sante Fe*) which turned violently and, streaming oil and smoke, headed back for Grytviken in South Georgia. *Brilliant*'s Lynx joined the Wessex in machine-gunning the submarine's casing. *Plymouth*'s Wasp and *Endurance*'s two Wasps were summoned to the scene and attacked with AS12 missiles. Badly damaged and unable to dive, *Santa Fe* managed to reach Grytviken but was abandoned in a sinking condition alongside the pier.

This, the Fleet Air Arm's first submarine kill since the Second World War, was the culmination of nearly forty years of training and preparation and it was achieved by three different types of helicopter using four different weapons: depth-charges, machine-guns, missiles – and a torpedo carried by *Brilliant*'s Lynx.

After a bombardment by the 4.5 inch guns of *Antrim* and *Plymouth* later that day, a seventy-five-strong party of Marines, SAS and SBS was landed by helicopter. The Argentinian defenders surrendered. The formal surrender of South Georgia was signed on board *Antrim* on 26 April.

Total Exclusion Zone

For the Task Force, now well down into the South Atlantic, the only 'hostile' action so far had been by a Boeing 707 with Argentine markings (and with Argentinian military observers on board) which approached the Task Force on 21 April and was intercepted by a Sea Harrier. Both sides took photographs.

To the men of the Task Force, the intense political activity at Westminster and at the United Nations, General Haig's shuttlings to and fro between London, New York and Buenos Aires, and the imposition of a 200-mile total exclusion zone around the Falklands, might all have been happening on another planet. Their sole contact with the outside world was the BBC World Service News and even there it seemed the Task Force had lately dropped from the headlines. But now, suddenly, with the news from South Georgia, it seemed this might be a shooting war after all.

All doubts were removed on 1 May by the first (of an eventual five) sortie of Operation BLACK BUCK, when an RAF Vulcan bomber of 101 Squadron, armed with twenty-one 1,000 lb bombs, flew from Ascension to bomb the runway of Port Stanley airfield. The sixteen-hour, 7,860 mile round trip, involving six in-flight refuellings and ten supporting Victor tankers of 55 and 57 Squadrons, was at that time the longest operational bombing mission ever flown. The damage done by the single runway hit achieved was not great but it had a considerable psychological effect on the Argentinians – and was very encouraging for the civilian population of Port Stanley.

Wrecked Wessex 5 helicopter on Fortuna Glacier, South Georgia

Later the same day, Sea Harriers of 800 Squadron armed with cluster bombs destroyed an Islander aircraft on Port Stanley runway and a Pucará at Goose Green. At 4.30 pm local time (7.30 pm for the Task Force, who kept Greenwich Mean Time throughout), a Mirage closing the Task Force north of West Falkland was shot down by a Sidewinder missile fired from a Sea Harrier of 801 Squadron.

This was the first ever kill by a Sea Harrier, and it was accomplished by an RAF pilot, Flight Lieutenant Barton. Another Mirage, badly damaged by a Sea Harrier's Sidewinder in the same engagement, tried to land at Port Stanley and was shot down by 'friendly' gunfire. Sea Harriers went on to shoot down a Dagger and a Canberra in this first and very successful day for them.

Flt Lt Dave Morgan, highest
scorer of the Sea Harrier pilots
and (opposite) Sea Harrier with
bomb racks empty landing on
HMS *Hermes* after a mission
over Port Stanley

The Argentinian 'own goal' on the Mirage was actually seen from the destroyer *Glamorgan* and the frigates *Arrow* and *Alacrity* which were carrying out a bombardment of the airfield, with spotting corrections from their own helicopters. A flight of four Daggers then bombed and strafed the ships. *Glamorgan* was shaken by two 500 lb bomb near-misses, one on each side of her quarterdeck, while *Arrow* suffered structural damage and one casualty from splinters and 30 mm cannon shells. These, the first air attacks on British warships since 1945, were a most uncomfortable and ominous foretaste of things to come.

The ships withdrew, but returned to the gunline later to complete the bombardment, against some counter-battery fire. Although these ships were to be hard-worked on naval gunfire support, their second bombardment, planned for the next day, was cancelled. Other events intervened.

The bulk of the Argentine Navy, designated Task Force 79, was now at sea, with the main body, including the carrier *25 de Mayo* in TG 79.1, north-west of the Falklands, searching for the British Task Force. The other half of the planned 'pincer' was Task Group 79.3: the cruiser *General Belgrano*, with two destroyers and an oiler, south of the Falklands.

At 11.30 pm on 1 May, a Tracker from *25 de Mayo* detected the British Task Force as one large and six medium-sized contacts, 300

miles to the east. TGs 79.1 and 79.2 steamed east during the night intending to launch a strike of eight A–4 Skyhawks armed with bombs at dawn. But, unusually for the area, the day was calm with very light winds.

Although *25 de Mayo* had a steam catapult and could make 25 knots, at least theoretically, and although the news of the attacks on Port Stanley meant that TF 79 was effectively at war and risks should be taken, the Argentinian commander Rear Admiral Luis Lombardo decided the Skyhawks could not take off successfully with enough range and bomb-load in such light wind conditions. He did not even stand on to the east, to close the range and hope that the wind would get up later in the day. Rather lamely, he took his ships away to the west, to await a second chance – which never came. His golden chance was gone for ever.

Both Argentinian task groups had been detected, Lombardo's ships by a Sea Harrier from *Invincible*, while the nuclear submarine *Conqueror* was in contact with the cruiser to the south, whose tasks were to provide early warning of a British approach to southern Argentina and to intercept any possible British reinforcements from the Pacific.

The presence of *General Belgrano*, whether or not she was inside the exclusion zone and whatever course she was steering, taken with the known threat from the north, constituted a danger to the Task Force.

For the first and only time, Admiral Woodward requested an extension of the Rules of Engagement, which was granted. At about 4 pm on 2 May, *General Belgrano* was hit on her port side by two Mark 8 torpedoes from *Conqueror* and sank with the loss of 321 of her people. In the British ships, the initial elation of the news soon faded, giving way to regret at the loss of life, coupled with the feeling that 'it might have been us'.

The shock of that sinking had a dramatically chastening effect upon the Argentinian Navy, whose major warships took no further part in the conflict. In the British ships, there could be no remaining doubts that this was now a real shooting war and violent action could come to anybody at any time.

In the dark hours of 2 May, a Sea King of 826 Squadron detected a radar contact at sea north of the Falklands. It was one of two Argentinian patrol craft (actually searching for the crew of the Canberra shot down a day earlier) which fired on the Sea King. The destroyer *Coventry*'s Lynx helicopter was called to the scene and launched her two Sea Skua missiles, at about eight miles range. Both hit the Argentinian *Comodoro Somellera*, and sank her.

Shortly afterwards, *Glasgow*'s Lynx fired her Sea Skuas at the second patrol craft, *Alferez Sobral*, which struggled back to harbour, badly damaged and with several casualties, a week later. This was a most satisfactory outcome for *Coventry* and *Glasgow* and for the Sea Skua, which was a new weapon.

Marines from 40 Commando on *Hermes'* flight deck

On 2 May, the Argentinian Navy planned to attack the British Task Force with two Super Etendards, armed with AM–39 French-built Exocet air-to-surface missiles, flying from the airfield at Rio Grande (the Super Etendards were not qualified for deck landings on *25 de Mayo*). But the KC–130 tanker for in-flight refuelling went unserviceable and the mission was aborted. On 4 May, they tried again. This time, they scored a shot which rang around the world, with implications which were to reverberate through the Royal Navy for years to come.

Exocet!

Tuesday 4 May was a bad day for the Task Force. Early that morning three Sea Harriers of 800 Squadron bombed Goose Green. Lieutenant Nick Taylor was attacking parked Pucarás on the airstrip with cluster bombs when his Harrier was hit by ground fire, burst into flames, flew on for some way, and then crashed in a huge ball of fire. Taylor did not eject and must have been killed almost instantly. This was the first Sea Harrier to be shot down. There were no more such low-level attacks against defended targets.

Meanwhile, an Argentinian maritime reconnaissance Neptune P–2 had detected ships of the Task Force about 100 miles south of Port Stanley. At 9.45 am local time (12.45 pm GMT or Task Force time) two Super Etendards piloted by Lieutenant Commander Augusto Bedacarratz and Lieutenant Armando Mayora took off from Rio Grande, each carrying an AM–39 Exocet (which the Task Force's intelligence had not so far believed they were capable of doing). After fifteen minutes, the Super Etendards refuelled in flight (another capability which intelligence had not appreciated) and, guided by sporadic reports from the Neptune, flew at 50 feet above the waves towards the Task Force.

Just before 2 pm (Task Force time), when the Super Etendards were closing the Task Force rapidly from the south-west, they pulled up to about 120 feet and switched on radar to search for their targets. They were immediately detected by the destroyer *Glasgow* at forty miles range and by *Invincible* at fifty miles.

Glasgow could hardly have been expected to identify the incoming 'bogies' at once as Super Etendards armed with Exocet missiles (especially as Super Etendards previously 'identified' had proved to be Mirages). After some understandable hesitation, *Glasgow* gave an alert and later fired 'chaff' (to distract a missile's radar). But her alarm was rather 'pooh-poohed' for lack of 'collateral' confirmation. The destroyer *Sheffield*, the nearest ship which could have provided collateral, was then acting as radar picket, one of three air defence ships, some twenty miles north-west of the main body and about seventy miles south-east of Port Stanley. But unfortunately she happened to be using a satellite transmitter at the time, which 'blinded' her main air-guard radar.

Super Etendard taking off from the Argentinian carrier *25 de Mayo* (below)

But at 2.10, *Sheffield* herself detected two contacts on her starboard bow, range twenty miles, and classified them as Mirages. A minute later, one of the contacts turned towards her, apparently on a visual sighting, but there is no evidence that the Argentinian pilot positively identified his target. In this most chillingly impersonal type of warfare, he literally fired and then left.

Sheffield's Officer of the Watch actually saw one contact, trailing black smoke, about six to eight miles away on the starboard bow, and identified it as a missile.

The Exocet approached *Sheffield* from an angle of about 40 degrees on her starboard bow and, a few seconds before 2.14 pm, hit her starboard side amidships, some six feet above the waterline.

The impact was surprisingly mild. Captain 'Sam' Salt was in his cabin, writing up his diary, when he heard 'one bang, not spectacular at all, which actually sounded like the 20 mm Oerlikon above my cabin going off'. The warhead very probably did not detonate, but the kinetic energy of a half-ton missile brought to rest from over 600 mph in the space of a few feet did massive damage to *Sheffield*'s structure, while unburnt rocket fuel caused a major fire, accompanied by clouds of dense black smoke which rapidly filled much of the midships portion of the ship's hull.

There was, in Salt's words, 'an extraordinary silence'. But, in the seconds it took Salt to get up there, the smoke had already reached the bridge; fifty per cent of ship's power had failed: all communications, internal and to other ships, had been lost; the one pump supplying the firemain had stopped and there was no water for fire-fighting; the impenetrable smoke, not only acrid but actually lethal, hampered damage control. Some sailors used anti-gas respirators, which had only a limited value in smoke, and at least one life was thereby lost.

Below decks, there were some distressing scenes. One sailor heard his friend, who did not survive, shouting, screaming and hammering against a jammed bulkhead door. The ship's galley had been in the direct path of the rocket and virtually the whole galley staff were killed. The crew of the computer room nearby, held at their posts to the end by the sheer willpower and discipline exerted by the officer in charge of them, died where they sat.

For some time *Sheffield*'s ship's company, with admirable coolness, continued to fight the fires raging forward and amidships. They were ably assisted by *Arrow*, who came alongside to lend hoses and manpower. At one point it did seem the fires might be put out. But after four hours, Salt realized that the forward decks were now actually hot underfoot and the fire was only one small compartment, where the bulkhead paint was already blistering, away from the Sea Dart missile magazine. At about 6.45 pm, Salt gave the order to abandon ship.

The smoke cloud of the Exocet hit had been seen on the horizon from *Hermes*' bridge where, as in the rest of the Task Force, the first reaction was one of disbelief. Then it was thought that *Sheffield* had suffered an internal explosion or, as submarines had been much on the Task Force's mind in the clear weather that day, she might have been torpedoed. Submarine contacts were detected and *Yarmouth* and *Arrow* began enthusiastically 'sardine-bashing' with depth charges. At 2.37 pm, *Yarmouth* reported seeing the second missile passing 1,000 yards down her starboard side.

It was hoped that the hulk of *Sheffield* might be saved. But at 7 am GMT on 11 May, when she was being towed out of the total exclusion zone in worsening weather, she suddenly rolled over and sank. She was the first British warship to be lost to air attack since the Second World War and her passing, with the loss of twenty-one of her ship's company, was a most profound shock, to the nation at home and to the men of the Task Force. In the liner *Canberra*, coming south with the 3rd Commando Brigade embarked, 'it was as if the temperature had dropped by ten degrees'. In *Sheffield*'s sister ship *Coventry*, hardly a word was spoken on board for twenty-four hours. In *Hermes*, Admiral Woodward (who had once commanded the 'Shiny Sheff' himself) and his staff were badly shocked. Eventually, Woodward had, as he later said, 'consciously to pull myself together and say "Really I've got to get on with the war".'

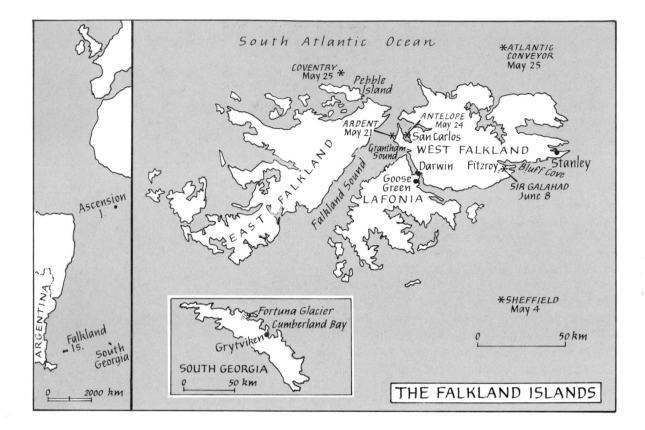

The Falkland Islands

War of Attrition

For the ships, 'getting on with the war' meant night bombardments 'to keep the Argies awake', insertions of parties of SAS and SBS at points along the coast, maintaining a surface ship blockade around the island and, above all, attempting to wear down the Argentinian Air Force.

Some Argentinian air losses were self-inflicted, as when two Skyhawks flew into a cliff on South Jason Island on 9 May and another was shot down by gunfire at Goose Green on 12 May. *Coventry*'s Sea Dart shot down an Army Puma helicopter near Port Stanley on 9 May (the first ever kill for this missile). At the time, the Type 42 destroyer *Coventry* was in company with the Type 22 frigate *Broadsword*, both in a newly-devised type of small group, known as a '22/42 Combo', formed for mutual anti-aircraft defence and to 'trail a coat and generally spoil the Argies' day'.

The first Sea Wolf kills were achieved off Port Stanley on 12 May by another '22/42 Combo' of *Glasgow* and *Brilliant*, whose Sea Wolf shot down two Skyhawks, and a third crashed into the sea while evading a missile. But *Glasgow* was hit by a 1,000 lb bomb which passed through her after engine room, without exploding until it was clear. Unexploded Argentinian bombs were, arguably, to be a main factor in keeping the Falkland Islands British.

At sea, aircraft supported the blockade. On 9 May, Sea Harriers of 800 Squadron bombed and strafed the trawler *Narval*, which was being used as an intelligence-gatherer by the Argentinians. She was abandoned, boarded by a party from *Invincible*, but later sank. On 16 May, Sea Harriers of 800 Squadron bombed and strafed the freighters *Bahia Buen Suceso*, alongside a jetty at Fox Bay in West Falkland, and *Rio Carcarana*, in Falkland Sound; both were abandoned by their crews.

Eleven aircraft – six Pucarás, four Turbo-Mentors, and one Skyvan – were destroyed in an SAS raid on Pebble Island early on 15 May, to make a total of twenty-seven Argentinian aircraft and helicopters lost through various causes since the conflict began.

Extra fighters for the Task Force arrived on 18 May in the converted Ro-Ro (roll on/roll off) ship *Atlantic Conveyor*; six Harrier GR.3s of No. 1 (F) Squadron RAF and four Sea Harriers of the newly-formed 809 Squadron joined *Hermes*, and the other four Sea Harriers of 809 went to *Invincible*. But Argentinian air power was by no means subdued, and local air superiority was far from secure, when the main landing took place at San Carlos Bay on 21 May, and the longest and hardest day of air versus sea fighting since the Second World War began.

San Carlos

By nightfall on 20 May, the invasion fleet had assembled north of the Falklands. It was a motley armada, of some forty warships, RFAs and ships taken up from trade (STUFTs), but it was nevertheless an astonishing and moving sight which none of those there had ever expected to see.

There was *Canberra*, the 'Great White Whale', and the long black hull and white superstructure of the North Sea ferry *Norland*, with 2 Para embarked, and the bright red of Townsend Thoresen's *Europic Ferry*, with equipment for 2 Para, 29 Battery Royal Artillery and 656 Squadron Army Air Corps.

There was the assault ship *Fearless*, flying the broad pennant of Commodore Amphibious Warfare, Commodore M.C. Clapp, with 3rd Commando Brigade HQ and 40 Commando embarked, and her sister ship *Intrepid*, with 3 Para on board.

There was the RFA *Stromness*, with 45 Commando, and the five RFA 'Sir' landing ships, all crammed with troops and their equipment. Astern to the east were the two carriers, only grey shadowy shapes in the mist. Lynx helicopters flew overhead, with the occasional Sea Harrier and, far out on the horizon, Sea Kings with 'dipping' sonar, searching for submarines.

At 11.30 pm, the fleet split into three. The carrier group and escort remained at sea, to provide air cover, while the *Fearless* group and the landing ship group steamed as stealthily as their sizes and appearances permitted, and in visibility which fortunately for them was very poor, to carry out Operation SUTTON –

the landing on East Falkland. There was, as in Nelson's day, a shortage of escorts – only one destroyer, *Antrim*, and six frigates.

Fearless, with *Antrim*, *Ardent*, *Intrepid*, *Yarmouth*, *Plymouth*, *Norland*, *Canberra*, and the RFAs *Stromness* and *Fort Austin* entered Falkland Sound just after midnight, anchored one and a half miles off Chancho Point, at the entrance to San Carlos Water, and were landing their troops by 2.30 am on 21 May. The landing ships, led by *Sir Percivale*, with *Sir Lancelot*, *Sir Galahad*, *Sir Tristram*, and *Sir Geraint*, followed by *Europic Ferry*, and escorted by *Broadsword*, *Brilliant*, and *Argonaut*, arrived in the Sound at 9.30.

By noon GMT (9 am local time), the first landing phase was complete, the nearest shores had been secured, and the RFAs, except *Fort Austin*, and the STUFTs moved into San Carlos Water to carry on unloading. Meanwhile, the warships disposed themselves in a 'gunline' across the entrance to San Carlos and along Falkland Sound, to await the counter-attacks they knew must come. The clouds had rolled away, and it was a day of bright sunshine and crystal clear visibility – perfect for attacking aircraft.

Yet, strangely, there was no enemy reaction until just after 10 am (local time) when a reconnaissance Pucará reported twelve ships in San Carlos. Five minutes later, a solitary Macchi 339 from Port Stanley flew low into San Carlos and its pilot, Lieutenant Crippa, suddenly saw what to him 'looked like the entire British fleet'. Crippa attacked *Argonaut* with 5 inch rockets and 30 mm cannon fire, causing upperdeck damage and some casualties.

The first attack from the mainland was half an hour later, when six Daggers arrived to carry out an armed reconnaissance of the area where the British ships had been reported. They saw *Antrim*, *Broadsword* and *Argonaut* out in the Sound and attacked with 1,000 lb bombs and cannon fire. All three ships suffered minor damage and casualties, and *Antrim* was also hit by one 1,000 lb bomb which lodged in her stern but did not explode. One Dagger was shot down by Sea Cat missiles fired from *Argonaut* and *Plymouth*.

This set the pattern for that hectic day. The Argentinian pilots flew with a skill and ferocious gallantry which surprised their opponents. Indeed they flew too well, pressing home their attacks to such close ranges that their bombs had not enough time in free flight to arm themselves, so that a large proportion failed to explode on impact.

The attackers were also ill-advised in their choice of targets, concentrating upon the escorts in the Sound, while the large ships in San Carlos Water, such as *Canberra* (which Admiral Woodward sombrely described as 'a floating bonfire awaiting a light'), were comparatively unscathed. The ships carrying the troops, the munitions and the equipment for the reconquest of the Falklands should have been the primary targets.

The 'Great White Whale'. The
liner *Canberra*, converted to a
troop ship with helipads in
place, on her way to the
Falklands

But this pattern was not obvious to either attackers or defenders
on the day. Once the Argentinians had realized that the landing at
San Carlos was in earnest, their Mirages, Daggers and Skyhawks
from the mainland began to arrive in waves of up to six aircraft,
skimming at 30 feet above the still waters of the Sound. Their
wings flashed a sudden warning silver in the sunlight as they
banked and approached for their attacking runs below masthead
height.

The ships replied with all the armament they had. The nearby
hillsides echoed and re-echoed to the screaming howl of jet
engines, the thumping and thudding of Bofors and Oerlikon anti-
aircraft guns, and the rattle of the scores of extra upperdeck
GPMGs (general purpose machine-guns) with which the ships had
been fitted. From time to time, there was the characteristic rushing
and tearing sound, like a giant cloth torn in two, of a missile being
fired. Thousand pound bombs detonated between the ships, sometimes so close that the great columns of water spouting up seemed
to hang in the air for minutes, before drifting as spray across the
nearest decks. Overhead, the clear sky was scored with missile
smoke trails and pockmarked with the brown, grey and black
smudges of exploding shells.

As the long day wore on and, despite their losses, the Argentinian jets returned again and again to the attack, it became
clear that the Royal Navy's post-war theories of air warfare were

being literally blown away. As in the Pacific in 1945, the Navy's ships simply did not have the weight of fire power to protect themselves against determined close-range air attack.

Brilliant's Sea Wolf surface-to-air missile system had worked adequately out in the Sound. But in San Carlos, surrounded by hills, with its radar confused by 'clutter' and its computer overwhelmed by hundreds of inputs, Sea Wolf 'gave up'. 'The only other firepower we had on this almost brand new ship,' said *Brilliant's* commanding officer, Captain John Coward, 'were two absolutely useless Bofors, built in Canada in 1942!'

With their own radar sets masked by the hills of San Carlos, and the Task Force itself having no long-range early warning radar, many ships discovered that the earliest and most reliable warnings of approaching aircraft were from that old-fashioned and supposedly obsolete sensor, the 'Mark One human eyeball'. Men with sharp eyesight were suddenly worth their weight in gold.

Had all the Argentinian bombs exploded properly, the day would have been a disaster for the escorts. As it was, the day went quite badly enough. *Ardent* had been deliberately placed in the most exposed station of all, in Grantham Sound, where earlier in the day she had given gunfire support to an SAS operation at Goose Green. *Ardent's* position in the Sound was almost directly under the flight path of aircraft approaching and leaving the battle area and she was subjected to several bombing and strafing attacks during the day.

Ardent defended herself stoutly with Sea Cat missiles, her 4.5 inch gun, Oerlikons and small arms fire (which, manned by her NAAFI canteen manager, assisted in the shooting down of at least one Skyhawk) but she was hit during a Dagger attack at about 2.30 pm by a 1,000 lb bomb which exploded in the area of the hangar. Heroic damage control saved the situation and the ship, but *Ardent* was hit again in a Skyhawk attack fifteen minutes later and a third time in another with 500 lb 'Snakeye' bombs just after 3 pm. She had suffered such serious damage that she was abandoned, with the loss of twenty-two lives, and later sank.

Against such dedicated air attacks, it was necessary literally to blow the incoming aircraft out of the sky, and this the small ships were not equipped to do. *Broadsword* and *Brilliant* were both damaged in close-range strafing attacks. *Argonaut*, which had suffered the first attack of the day, was hit twice by 1,000 lb bombs from Skyhawks in the afternoon. Neither bomb exploded, but the ship was still very badly damaged and might have become a total loss but for a quick-witted sub-lieutenant on the fo'c'sle who anchored the ship before she drifted ashore, out of control, on Fanning Head.

Despite the strenuous efforts of the BBC to enlighten them, the Argentinians did not appear to realize the failures of their bombs for some time. In San Carlos Water, on 23 May, another frigate – *Antelope* – was hit by two 1,000 lb bombs, neither of which exploded. But one bomb detonated while it was being defused. The ship burned out and sank. The following day, 24 May, in San Carlos Water, *Sir Galahad, Sir Lancelot* and *Sir Bedivere* suffered moderate or minor damage when they were all hit by 1,000 lb bombs which failed to explode. Thus, of the ten 1,000 lb bombs which had scored direct hits since the attack on *Glasgow* on 12 May, only one (*Ardent*) detonated correctly on impact.

Whilst the ship's companies of the escorts manned their guns and anxiously scanned the sky, or waited below decks devoutly hoping that the explosions they could hear were unconnected with their own ship, they could have been excused for wondering where were their own aircraft.

In fact, the Sea Harriers had not been idle, having established since dawn CAPs of two aircraft each, concentrating upon three main areas: north of the islands, over West Falkland, and at the southern entrance to the Sound to catch Argentinian aircraft flying homewards after their missions. *Brilliant*'s Sea Wolf radar may have failed the ship herself but proved very useful here for fighter direction.

The first success was by three Sea Harriers of 801 Squadron which shot down a Pucará over Darwin with 30 mm cannon fire. But the most successful weapon by far was the Sidewinder AIM–9L air-to-air missile, with which Sea Harriers of 800 and 801 Squadrons shot down four Daggers and three Skyhawks over West Falkland or the Sound during the day.

HMS *Antelope* blowing up in San Carlos Bay when a bomb
lodged in the ship's engine room exploded while a bomb
disposal team was attempting to defuse it

Atlantic Conveyor abandoned and burning
after an Exocet missile hit port side aft

RFA *Sir Bedivere* seen through the gun
sight of an attacking Argentinian Dagger,
San Carlos Water, 25 May 1982

HMS *Hermes*, the Task Force flagship, with her escorting 'goalkeeper', the Type 22 frigate HMS *Broadsword*

In one brilliant little afternoon encounter, which summed up the Sea Harriers' day, Lieutenant Commander 'Sharkey' Ward, CO of 801 Squadron, and Lieutenant S. Thomas, saw a pair of eastbound Daggers north of Port Howard, West Falkland. 'I barrelled in behind them,' said Thomas, 'locked up a missile on the rear guy and fired. The Sidewinder hit the aircraft and took it apart. I didn't see it go in. I was busy trying to get the other one. He went into a climbing turn to starboard to try to get away. I locked up the Sidewinder and fired it. The missile followed him round the corner and went close over his port wing root. There was a bright orange flash . . .'

Whilst watching this, Ward saw a third Dagger fly west past his nose. 'He seemed to be nothing to do with the other two, he came from a different direction. He was very low, about half a mile ahead of me and going very fast. He was doing about 500 knots at fiftyish feet. I just racked the Sea Harrier round hard, called Steve to say I'd got a third one, and loosed off a missile. It hit him and immediately afterwards he went into the ground. I remember seeing the leading edge of the starboard wing cart-wheeling away.'

Those three Daggers were part of a total of fifteen Argentinian aircraft lost by various causes on 21 May. They included three helicopters strafed and destroyed on the ground at Mount Kent by RAF Harriers of No. 1 Squadron, and a Pucará shot down in the Sussex Mountains by an enterprising SAS man with a Stinger infra-red homing missile fired from the shoulder.

On the other side, two Royal Marine Gazelle helicopters were shot down by small arms fire soon after the San Carlos landing, an RAF Harrier was shot down by ground fire at Port Howard, and *Ardent*'s Lynx was lost with the ship. But, by the end of that day, more than 3,000 troops were ashore, and the beach-heads had been consolidated.

25 May

The landing at San Carlos had taken the Argentinians utterly by surprise, but their Air Force had reacted swiftly and forcefully. They had already achieved more against an opposing navy than any other air arm since 1945. There were lessons to be learned from the day. It would be better, even now, to go for the large ships than for the escorts – and the quicker the better, before Rapier and Blowpipe surface-to-air missile defences could be properly established ashore. But even the escorts were clearly vulnerable. If the air attacks could be synchronized, and made from different directions simultaneously, the escorts' defences could be swamped.

Everything cried out for a renewed and even greater effort by the Argentinians on 22 May. But, curiously, there was a lull. Operational defects, bad weather over the southern air bases, a long pause for consideration of what tactics to pursue next, and possibly shock over the losses of the previous day, meant there was

HMS *Coventry* rolling over after three bomb hits

no air activity at San Carlos until the evening when a pair of Skyhawks dropped bombs fruitlessly and escaped.

There was one other factor: the Sea Harrier seemed already to have established a kind of psychological ascendancy over its opponents. '.... I thought we had escaped,' said Lieutenant Commander Philippi, one of the Skyhawk pilots who bombed *Ardent*, 'when a shout from Marquez froze my heart: "Harrier! Harrier!" I immediately ordered the tanks and bomb racks to be jettisoned in the hope we would be able to reach the safety of the cloud ahead of us.' But Philippi did not escape; his Skyhawk was hit by a Sidewinder, and he had to eject.

No Harrier was lost in air-to-air combat, but there were operational losses. One of the saddest and certainly the most dramatic, happening in full view of the flagship, was the death of Lieutenant Commander 'Gordy' Batt of 800 Squadron. He had already flown twenty-nine operational sorties when, on the night of 23 May, he led a flight of four Sea Harriers from *Hermes* to attack Port Stanley airfield, but crashed soon after take-off.

'I saw this great yellow flash lasting about three seconds go across low down on the horizon,' said Admiral Woodward, who had known Batt well. 'I suspect he lost his orientation and fell into the water. Certainly it looked as though it was bits of aeroplane burning rapidly for three or four seconds before it went out – just like a light. You knew you had just seen somebody die, but because it was dark and distant there was a grotesque unreality about it.'

On 25 May, Argentina's National Day, the eponymous carrier did not appear, but the Air Force did. Just after 3 pm, four Skyhawks from Rio Gallegos attacked the 'Combo' of *Coventry* and *Broadsword* which, with their combination of Sea Dart and Sea Wolf, were stationed as a 'missile trap' north of Pebble Island.

As *Broadsword*'s Second Officer of the Watch later recorded, matters did not go quite as expected. 'Suddenly we detected aircraft closing. Sea Harriers were in the area but, no problem, Sea Dart would take out the attackers. Any moment now, *Coventry* would fire. Still, the aircraft were *very* close.

'"AIRCRAFT VISUAL! VERY LOW! GREEN NINE ZERO!"

'The aircraft were so low the water sprayed up behind them. *Coventry* still did not fire but still no problem, we'll get them with Sea Wolf . . .Any moment now . . . Why have we not fired? The Skyhawks roar over the top. I saw the bombs dropping down aft . . . Still have steering, there was no big bang, breathe again, we must be OK.

'"AIRCRAFT CLOSING! RIGHT AHEAD!"

'This time we'll get them. They were going for *Coventry*, we had locked-on – Come on Seawolf!

'"COVENTRY'S TURNING IN OUR WAY!"

'She turned right in front of us and, unable to fire, we could only watch as two more Skyhawks screamed over the top. *Coventry* was hit and exploded seconds later, sending a cloud of debris high into the air.'

Broadsword had been hit aft by one bomb which did not explode. But the three bombs which hit *Coventry* did explode, and brought the ship to a standstill, all power lost. *Coventry* turned over and sank quickly, taking with her nineteen of her people. In a very short time, all that was left was a cluster of red dinghies, and rescue helicopters already hovering overhead.

Thus, ironically, of the three Type 42 destroyers, whose main *raison d'être* was air defence, *Sheffield* and *Coventry* had been sunk and *Glasgow* had been damaged – all by air attack. They might or might not be able to protect the fleet with Sea Dart. They certainly could not protect themselves.

The Argentinians were well aware that if only they could sink or badly damage the carriers, or just one carrier, the war would be virtually over. On 25 May, when, as it happened, the carrier group had moved nearer, to a position only some 130 miles east of the Falklands, to give the Sea Harriers more sortie time over the islands, the Argentinian Navy tried again.

Two Exocet-armed Super Etendards, piloted by Lieutenant Commander Roberto Curilovic and Lieutenant Julio Barraza, took off from Rio Grande at 2.30 pm and, after refuelling in flight, flew 120 miles north of the Falklands, to approach the estimated position of the carrier group from the north. Once again, they located their targets, fired at the biggest of the contacts, turned and withdrew.

Argentinian Mirage dodging anti-aircraft fire from British ships

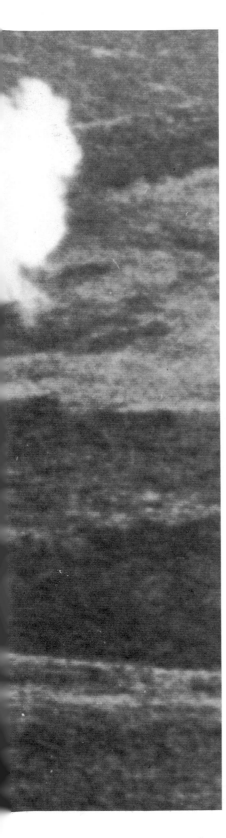

The Exocets may well have been accurately aimed at *Hermes* and *Invincible*, in the middle of the group, but the carrier group had learned from *Sheffield*'s experience. As soon as the Etendards switched on their radars for the briefest moment to search for the targets, and the telltale Exocet radar 'racket' was detected, ships and helicopters put into effect an improved routine, firing 'chaff' guns and other devices for decoying missiles.

They were partially successful. One missile ran on and missed. But the other was deflected towards the Ro-Ro ship *Atlantic Conveyor*. She was turning hard to port, conforming to the task group's general missile evasion manoeuvring, but the Exocet impacted upon her port quarter, about ten feet above the water-line, and started a huge fire inside the hull. 'Only 20 minutes after being hit,' said Captain Layard, the senior naval officer on board, 'it was clear that our ship was doomed and all our attempts to quell the fires were to no avail.'

The fire was creeping forward, towards thousands of gallons of stored kerosene and racks of cluster bombs 'which could blow us to pieces at any moment'. The upper deck was already too hot to stand on. The ship's captain, Ian North (who had twice been sunk in the Second World War) gave the order to abandon ship. *Atlantic Conveyor* did not sink until 30 May, but twelve of her ship's company were lost, Ian North among them.

Also lost were six Wessex, three Chinooks and one Lynx, and a large quantity of spare parts and other stores such as thousands of tents, numerous vehicles, and metal strips for building temporary runways – all items which were to be sorely missed in the weeks to come.

But, by 25 May, over 5,500 troops and 5,000 tons of supplies, armaments and equipment were ashore. The 'long yomp', which was to end in Port Stanley, began with the break-out from the beach-head on 27 May.

30 May

With the steady yomping progress of the Commandos across East Falkland, the stunning bravery of Colonel 'H' and his Paras at Goose Green, the arrival of *QE2* with the Guards and the Gurkhas of 5th Infantry Brigade, and the ubiquitous, vital helicopters which provided a buzzing accompaniment to every television screen image, the media tended to turn their main attention away from the carrier group.

But the Argentinians had certainly not forgotten the carriers. They were still the key to victory. A long-range radar installation near Port Stanley was providing valuable information from which the carrier group's position and daily movements could be estimated. Shortly after midday (local time) on 30 May, two Super Etendards took off from Rio Grande. The leader, flown by Lieutenant Commander Francisco, was armed with the sole remaining

Exocet missile. The other, flown by Lieutenant Collavino, carried an extra radar pod in lieu of a missile.

The Etendards were accompanied by four A–4 Skyhawks, each armed with two 500 lb bombs and each flown by a volunteer. The Skyhawks, having no search radar, would keep station on the Etendards visually. The six aircraft, refuelling in flight, would fly 100 miles south of the Falklands to a point where it was estimated they would be south of the carrier group. They then descended to 100 feet and flew north for the Etendards' radar to locate the targets. After the Exocet was fired, the Super Etendards wheeled away and headed for home, while the Skyhawks followed the missile's smoke trail in towards the carriers for a close-range, low-level bombing attack.

HMS *Brilliant*'s Lynx arriving to pick up stores from HMS *Hermes*' flight deck

It was a reasonable plan, and it might have worked – indeed, the Argentinian Air Force insists to this day that it did work. The Super Etendards pulled up very briefly three times during the approach to check the targets. Francisco fired at a range of just over thirty miles, at a target to the north-west.

Visibility was about nine miles in thin fog banks, and it was at this range that the Skyhawks following the missile sighted *Invincible*. She was steering south-west, apparently alone with no escort, and the Skyhawks were approaching her, it seemed without having been detected themselves, from about thirty degrees on her port quarter.

It was an alert frigate, *Ambuscade*, that first picked up the Exocet 'racket' and reported the missile release. It was also detected by another frigate, *Avenger*, which was then some twenty miles south of the main group, on passage with the destroyer *Exeter* to the Falklands to carry out a bombardment and land special forces that evening.

Avenger's ship's company heard the ominous pipe 'Impact imminent 12 seconds! Brace, Brace, BRACE!' and the prolonged roar of gunfire, Sea Dart missiles, and bomb explosions. The ship's 4.5 inch gun actually picked off the Exocet missile in flight – the sole kill by this weapon during the conflict. 'You may be interested to know that the Exocet was only nine kilometres out when we hit it,' Captain Hugo White informed his listeners. 'I don't need to tell you that at Mach 1 that is not very many seconds. I told you when we left Guzz that I was lucky, well here's proof of it.' With that thought, *Avenger*'s sailors had to console themselves.

Meanwhile, *Exeter* had been restoring the Type 42's reputation by shooting down two of the incoming Skyhawks with her Sea Dart. From *Avenger*'s bridge they saw what Captain White called 'a nasty oily mess off our starboard beam'. A sea boat recovered some of one Skyhawk's remains: 'a sheepskin seat cover' which was actually a man's chest blown inside out, and a leg 'complete with flying suit and boot'. This was, in fact, as close as most of the sailors in the Task Force ever got to one of their enemies.

Two bombs exploded very close, either side of *Avenger*'s bows, but no damage was done and nobody was hurt. But one surviving Skyhawk pilot, Lieutenant Ureta, was sure he had hit *Invincible*. He said the Exocet also hit. He flew over the carrier, turned back, and saw black smoke rising from the superstructure. Ureta was believed by the Argentinian media who, understandably, made great propaganda play of his story.

Ships are notoriously difficult to identify from the air. Looking from astern, in poor visibility and gunsmoke, and in the heat and excitement of the attack, a frigate's helicopter platform could be mistaken for a flight deck. The smoke could have been from the funnel of a frigate manoeuvring violently to evade attack. Ureta very probably saw what he most desperately wanted to see. But neither *Invincible* nor *Hermes* was hit.

Endgame

During and after the conflict, Admiral Woodward was sul‚ected to a good deal of ill-informed criticism, some from those who should have known better, over his handling of the carriers. 'He was so far off to the east, he qualified for the Burma Star,' was one of the kinder remarks. In fact, as Woodward and his staff knew very well, the carriers were their most precious assets. Lose even one, and the war ended there and then. Because of Admiral Woodward's prudence, the carriers survived all attempts to sink them and provided air cover to the end, while events on East Falkland rolled on to their conclusion in the Argentinian surrender – which did not come a moment too soon for the battered ships of the Task Force – on 14 June.

There were still to be disasters and setbacks at sea before the end. *Plymouth*, one of the longest-serving and longest-suffering of frigates, was attacked by Daggers off San Carlos on 8 June and hit by four 1,000 lb bombs. None exploded, but the ship was badly damaged. A depth-charge on the flight deck was detonated by a cannon shell and started a serious fire.

On the same day, and at about the same time, Skyhawks found and attacked the RFA landing ships *Sir Galahad* and *Sir Tristram*, at anchor off Fitzroy Settlement in Port Pleasant. Both ships were bombed and very badly damaged, with many casualties among the ship's companies and the Welsh Guardsmen embarked, despite the most heroic rescue efforts of helicopters. *Sir Galahad* had to be scuttled and *Sir Tristram* was relegated to duty as an accommodation ship.

Exocet slung one last Parthian shot at about 3.30 am on 12 June, when *Glamorgan* had just completed a night bombardment in support of the final assault on Port Stanley and was retiring to rejoin the main group. The Exocet, fired from shore, was detected and a Sea Cat missile was fired at it, while *Glamorgan* took violent evasive action, and was actually turning hard to starboard when the missile hit her port side aft.

The warhead did not detonate, but the impact and fire devastated the hangar area and the main galley. The ship's company had fallen out from Action Stations five minutes earlier, or the casualties would have been much greater. As it was, thirteen men were killed and fourteen wounded.

By 14 June, the Argentinians had lost seventy aircraft, from the first Puma helicopter shot down by Royal Marines on South Georgia on the morning of 3 April to the final high-flying Canberra shot down by *Exeter*'s Sea Dart north of Port Stanley on the night of 13 June. Of these, Harriers accounted for thirty, shot down or destroyed on the ground, and surface missiles, guns and small arms for twenty. The highest scoring missile in the air was Sidewinder, with eighteen outright kills and a share of another. The best ship-borne missile was Sea Dart, with five kills – four of them by the sharp-shooting *Exeter* (whose Sea Dart also shot down a photo-reconnaissance Learjet over Pebble Island on 7 June). Another thirty-two Argentinian aircraft were captured when the islands were surrendered.

The top-scoring pilot was Flight Lieutenant David Morgan RAF, of 800 Squadron, with two Pumas, two Skyhawks and a half-share in an Augusta 109 helicopter. For the Harrier pilots, there was what Morgan called 'the victor's prerogative' of compassion. 'That part of the fight was now over,' he said. 'He had lost. I had won. He was no longer a threat and therefore I could afford to feel compassion for him.'

'It was just the success of shooting down the enemy air assets,' said 'Sharkey' Ward. 'That's what it was all about, and if a man survived, like the chap out of my Pucará survived – Major Tomba – *delighted*.'

The Task Force lost thirty-four aircraft, twenty-four of them helicopters – and ten of those were in *Atlantic Conveyor*. The next greatest number of losses – nine – were from 'operational accidents' for reasons varying from the Sea King of 846 Squadron abandoned near Punta Arenas in Chile on 20 May in circumstances still unexplained, to the Sea Harrier which slid off *Invincible*'s flight deck while the ship was turning in very bad weather on 29 May (the pilot, Lieutenant Commander Broadwater, ejected safely). Six Sea Harriers were lost, two to enemy action. Of four Harrier GR.3s of No. 1 Squadron lost, three were as

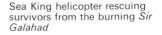

Sea King helicopter rescuing survivors from the burning *Sir Galahad*

The happy return: HMS
Invincible returning to
Portsmouth after the Falklands
conflict

a result of enemy ground-fire. Five Sea Kings were lost, all in operational accidents.

As a result of the Falklands experience, the Harrison Line mv *Astronomer* was converted into the helicopter support ship RFA *Reliant*, using the 'Arapaho' concept of adding a hangar, flight deck and accommodation to a container ship. With her five Sea Kings, *Reliant* was for months the forward operating base for ASW aircraft in the South Atlantic. In 1984 she went to the eastern Mediterranean where her helicopters supported the British peace-keeping force in the Lebanon.

An even more dramatic conversion is being carried out on the container ship *Contender Bezant* to transform her into the air training ship RFA *Argus*. With her flight deck, two aircraft lifts, operations room, and flying control, she will be a carrier in all but name. At 28,000 tons, she is bigger than the *Invincible* class and, with twelve Sea Harriers and six Sea Kings, carries more aircraft.

The Falklands conflict was the first missile war at sea, and it was one where, unlike the wars in Korea and Vietnam and the Suez operation, air power had been used at sea towards a clear political objective, which was successfully achieved. The war had many lessons for the Royal Navy. Captain L.E. Middleton, of *Hermes*, was almost the only officer in the Task Force who had seen previous combat, at Suez. A whole generation of naval officers had grown up with only peacetime exercise experience. For these, the Falklands illustrated the great gulf between peace and war: 'In an

exercise,' said one staff officer, 'you are always trying to achieve the best solution. In war, the best you can hope for is to retrieve the situation from catastrophe.'

In the years of peace, the Navy's ships had grown 'soft', with an understandably greater emphasis on habitability and living conditions; reporters who went down to the South Atlantic commented upon the difference between the pastel shades, mess-deck TV and gracious living of *Invincible*, and the craggier compartments and spartan layout of *Hermes*, a Second World War design.

The Falklands showed the need for much greater armament, in ships and in aircraft; long-range early warning radar; the importance of good and prompt damage control; the use of non-flammable materials for clothing and bedding; better breathing apparatus for fire-fighting; blast- and shatter-proof materials for ship's compartments and furnishings; more training in the repair of action damage to aircraft, and in the neglected art of fighter evasion by helicopters. Ships had to be painted a dull grey all over: even a funnel band gave an attacking aircraft an aiming mark.

When all the investigations had been made, all the inquiries held, and all the reasons and results deduced, digested and promulgated to the fleet, a curious similarity came to light. As one officer said, 'We were surprised, and even horrified, to find that the official lessons learned from the Falklands were *exactly* the same as the official lessons learned from World War Two!'

Showing the Flag

'GUNBOAT Diplomacy', so called, always required great political skill and judgement. To apply just enough local force, for just long enough to resolve a local political situation, involved a wide range of responses, varying from the 'flag-showing' appearance offshore of a minor war vessel, often literally a gunboat, to the landing of a full-scale expedition with troops and artillery.

Since the decline of the British Empire and the end of the Second World War, the policy has been carried on by the United States – which has not, it is fair to say, so far recaptured that precise Victorian finesse. The United States' flag-showing has met with particularly mixed success in the Mediterranean, where the US Sixth Fleet has been a vital prop for the southern bastion of NATO.

In 1945, there was one US Navy destroyer tender, berthed at Naples. The first small carrier group followed a year later. Forty years on, the Sixth Fleet's standard strength is about fifty ships, with at least one, sometimes two, and occasionally in times of tension three, large carrier battle groups on station.

But very gradually, over those forty years, the US Navy's status in the Mediterranean has changed from absolute supremacy to a state where the Red Navy has achieved a near parity.

The Six-Day Arab–Israeli War in June 1967 was the first time Soviet naval power was deployed extensively in a military crisis. Early in June, in advance of the crisis, the Soviets had sent ten additional ships from the Black Sea. Their Mediterranean Fleet strength eventually rose to more than seventy ships, including two cruisers, fifteen destroyers and ten submarines.

These ships took no actual part in the war, but Soviet ships often tried to harass and penetrate the escort screens of USS *Saratoga* and *America* carrier groups, passing close to and cutting sharply across American ships in a reckless and unseamanlike manner which endangered lives on both sides.

In the next crisis, over Jordan in September 1970, the Soviet naval reaction was more intense and used more sophisticated ships. Soviet strength built up to forty-nine ships, including ten submarines. The United States responded by sending a second carrier group, of USS *John F. Kennedy*, into the Mediterranean, and moving an amphibious task force east towards Jordan. The tension subsided after the Syrians invaded Jordan on 20 September and were defeated three days later.

The situation was resolved by the Jordanian Army before the Soviets had augmented their naval forces to the point where they confronted the Sixth Fleet. But the crisis had disturbing implications for the West, suggesting that the United States was so overstretched in the Mediterranean that it could not properly respond there if it were ever seriously challenged by the Soviet Navy. If, for instance, a large Soviet naval exercise in the eastern Mediterranean coincided with yet another crisis in the Middle East, the United States might find itself unable to support Israel.

The USS *Intrepid* passing through the Suez canal, June 1967

Both sides were still considering the political and military implications of the Jordanian crisis when, at noon on 6 October 1973, the Egyptian Army crossed the Suez Canal to open the Yom Kippur War. The Soviet Mediterranean Fleet at that time had fifty-two ships, including eleven submarines, three cruisers, six guided missile and conventional destroyers, with some frigates, minesweepers and two amphibious ships.

The Soviets (possibly with prior knowledge of the Egyptian assault) were carrying out a routine turnover of ships, and thus had another guided missile destroyer, four submarines and an auxiliary also in the Mediterranean. But the Soviets continued to reinforce their fleet throughout the war and, by 31 October, it had reached a peak of ninety-five ships, including two *Alligator* tank landing ships and five *Polnocny* medium landing ships capable of transporting 2,000 troops and their equipment.

The US Sixth Fleet, which also happened to be above its normal strength of forty-eight ships because of a recent amphibious exercise, had two aircraft carrier groups, USS *Independence* at

Athens and USS *Franklin D. Roosevelt*, in the western Mediterranean. There were also US amphibious forces at Suda Bay, in Crete.

The Soviets began a massive air and sea lift to replenish Egyptian losses. Their main surface fleet operated south of Crete, close to the Sixth Fleet flagship USS *Little Rock* and the *Independence* group. The Soviets increased their close-range surveillance and harassment of US ships and carried out anti-carrier warfare exercises. Because actual US carriers were the simulated targets, it was virtually impossible for the US ships to distinguish between an exercise and a real attack. The Soviet ships were all disposed in attack order, with weapons aimed. All that was needed was the order to fire.

By contrast, the American response was cautious to the point of timidity. They delayed their replenishment of Israel's losses, and when their airlift did begin, the Sixth Fleet Commander, Admiral Daniel Murphy, who had to provide surveillance, early radar warning and air-sea rescue, was forbidden to bring *Franklin D.*

One of the crew of the USS *Nimitz* (pictured opposite) jogging around her 4½-acre flight deck

Roosevelt's group east to join *Independence*. A third carrier group, USS *John F. Kennedy*, was ordered to remain to the west of Gibraltar. Murphy also had to keep his amphibious force at Suda Bay. He was unable to concentrate his fleet, and his ships stayed widely dispersed and vulnerable.

For some time, the fleets confronted each other, while the White House declared a heightened state of alert – Defence Condition Three (DEFCON 3) – for the first time since the Cuban crisis. This was in itself a political signal to the USSR, and was followed by an exchange of high-level notes, and a ceasefire in the war.

The two fleets were evenly matched. Probably the first to strike would have won. The Soviets were weak in aircraft and in anti-submarine warfare. But their surface and submarine missiles, launched in a pre-emptive attack, would cerainly have caused the Sixth Fleet severe loss and might have disabled or sunk *Independence*. In October 1973, the Soviet Navy posed its greatest ever threat to the US Navy which, for the first time since the war, was denied absolute control of the sea.

The changing balance of power at sea in the Middle East was accompanied by increasingly hostile sentiment ashore, most dramatically demonstrated by the violently anti-American revolution which overthrew the Shah of Iran in January 1979. On 4 November, about 400 militant Islamic students overran the United States embassy in Teheran and took sixty-six American citizens hostage.

Thirteen of the hostages were later released but the imprisonment of the remaining fifty-three was a continuing affront to American national pride. At last, in April 1980, goaded by the Iranians' triumphant crowing, the United States turned to sea power. A plan was evolved, code-named EAGLE CLAW, for a contingent of Rangers and Special Forces, known as Delta Force, to storm the US Embassy and rescue the hostages.

EAGLE CLAW required three MC–130 aircraft to carry Delta Force, three KC–130 fuel tankers, two C–130 gunships to overfly Teheran and quell any opposition, and two C–141 Starlifters with fighter cover for the final evacuation. These aircraft were to fly from the island of Mazirah off the coast of Oman.

Meanwhile, the carrier *Nimitz*, off the Gulf of Oman, was to launch eight RH–53D long-range Sea Stallions which would fly to Desert One, an airstrip some 300 miles south-east of Teheran, and wait for the signal that the hostages had been freed. The helicopters would then fly into Teheran, pick up the hostages from the embassy grounds or from a sports ground nearby and take them to a second desert rendezvous with the Starlifters. It was a fantastically complicated plan which would need good intelligence, good timing, good communications and, above all, good luck.

The eight helicopters took off from *Nimitz* on time at 1930 on 24 April. One helicopter suffered a serious mechanical defect and had to make a forced landing. Its crew were picked up and returned to *Nimitz*. The rescue could still go ahead; it had been decided that the safe minimum was six helicopters.

Fierce sandstorms caused two helicopters to land in the desert. Both took off again, but one had to return to *Nimitz* because of a defect. There was now no safety margin. When the helicopters finally arrived at Desert One, some over an hour late, yet another helicopter reported a defect which prevented it flying. With only five Sea Stallions left, the rescue had to be abandoned.

Worse was to come. As one Sea Stallion took off, it banked, slipped sideways and crashed into a KC–130 fuel tanker. Both burst into flames. Five of the tanker crew and three in the helicopter were killed. Another five men were injured. Delta Force had to return to Mazirah, having accomplished nothing.

There were those who were relieved, who felt that even if the rescue had been successful it would have caused more problems than it solved. But the news of the fiasco, the pictures of burned-out aircraft at Desert One, the public display of the eight American bodies in Teheran, and the propaganda mileage the gleeful Iranians made out of the whole disastrous affair were further affronts to American national self-esteem and undoubtedly contributed to Jimmy Carter's comprehensive defeat by Ronald Reagan in the following November.

The wreckage of the burnt-out Sea Stallion helicopter and KC–130 fuel tanker at Desert One after the disastrous attempt to rescue the American hostages in Teheran

Reagan's War

THE hostages were returned in January 1981, but Reagan soon had further problems in the Middle East. In 1973, Colonel Qaddafi had claimed the Gulf of Sirte as Libyan territorial waters. The Gulf was indisputably international water but in November 1979, during the Iranian hostage crisis, President Carter forbade the US Fleet to sail south of the latitude claimed by Qaddafi as his maritime frontier.

On 17 August 1981, two carrier groups, of USS *Forrestal* and *Nimitz*, carrying some 150 aircraft between them, sailed south into the Gulf of Sirte for exercises. Libyan intruders were detected by radar on seventy-two occasions in the next two days. But shortly after 0700 on the 19th, *Nimitz*'s radar and an airborne Hawkeye picked up two Soviet-built Su–22 (Fitter) fighters heading into the Gulf. As the Su–22s closed, they were intercepted by two Grumman F–14 Tomcats from the CAP.

The Su–22s were completely outclassed by the Tomcats, which were 300 mph faster and flown by the crack VF–41 'Black Ace' squadron from *Nimitz*, and they compounded their disadvantages with bad airmanship. The Su–22s fired one Atoll missile when the Tomcats were heading directly for them, although the Atoll is a heat-seeking missile much better fired from astern at the jet exhausts of its target. Having missed, the Su–22s passed beneath the Tomcats, banked steeply and fired a second missile.

Once fired on, the Tomcats could retaliate with their Side-winders. There was never any doubt about the outcome. One Su–22 exploded in flames. The second was hit by a missile which did not detonate and the pilot was seen to eject.

Whether or not the incident had been deliberate 'coat-trailing', the Pentagon was not unduly displeased with this show of American power. But Qaddafi only redoubled his anti-Americanism, claiming himself the champion of the Third World against American imperialism. Urged on by Qaddafi's inflammatory rhetoric and backed by his money, terrorism became a potent anti-American weapon.

While Libya and Syria both provided refuge, finance and training facilities for international terrorists, the outrages against American lives and property continued: more bombings against American diplomatic outposts, hijacked airliners on which any American passengers were always special targets, Americans seized as hostages on the street or in their homes, and 200 US marines killed in their sleep when a massive bomb demolished a barracks in Beirut.

In October 1985, four Palestinian gunmen hijacked the 24,000–ton Italian cruise liner *Achille Lauro*. One American passenger, Leon Klinghoffer, a 69-year-old invalid confined to a wheelchair, was murdered and his body thrown into the sea. American rage and frustration grew as, once again, it was demonstrated that the most powerful nation in the world was powerless to protect its citizens abroad.

Opposite above: The bright track of a missile lighting up the sky over Tripoli in the early hours of 15 April 1986
Below: An F–14 Tomcat aboard the USS *America*

The hijackers were given safe passage out of Egypt and, on 10 October, took off from a military airbase near Cairo in an Egyptian Boeing 737. The airliner was refused permission to land in Greece or in Tunisia but was south of Crete, flying west, apparently heading for Tunis when, towards midnight, six F–14 Tomcats ranged alongside and instructed the pilot by radio and by 'waggling wings' to head for Sicily.

The Tomcats, with EC2 Hawkeyes and KA–6 tankers, were from USS *Saratoga*, off the coast of Greece. The Boeing 737 had been tracked by radar since it left Cairo. It showed no sign of resistance, took no evasive action and landed at Sigonella NATO base in Sicily in the early hours of 11 October. Air power at sea had given the United States the chance, at last, to hit back at its tormentors.

Back home, the New York *Daily News* shrieking headline was 'We Bag the Bums!' 'It seems we finally did something right,' said one Congressman. 'It's about *time*,' said another, and the whole American nation jubilantly agreed. 'You can run,' said President Reagan, speaking with resonances of Wild West movies, 'but you can't hide.'

Unfortunately, this was not a film in which the good guys triumphed over the bad guys. In December 1985 there were terrorist bomb attacks at Rome and Vienna airports. Twenty people, including five Americans, were killed. In March 1986, three Sixth Fleet carrier groups, USS *Saratoga*, *America* and *Coral Sea*, with some 240 aircraft, and twenty-seven other ships, began an intentionally provocative exercise, Operation PRAIRIE FIRE, in waters off the Gulf of Sirte. At noon on the 24th, three US warships led by the nuclear-powered missile cruiser *Yorktown* crossed Qaddafi's 'Line of Death' drawn across the Gulf between Benghazi and Misratah.

For some weeks past, Libyan fighter pilots, and crews at the Ghurdabiyah missile base east of Sirte, had been reacting to radar detections of American ships and aircraft offshore. This had been a deliberate American policy, to keep the Libyans on edge. 'Every time they relaxed,' said one spokesman, 'we came right back at them.'

This time, two SA–5 missiles were fired from Ghurdabiyah at about 1400 and were followed later in the afternoon by four more missiles. All six missed. Libyan MiGs approached the Sixth Fleet and were headed off by the CAP. At about 2000, a Libyan patrol boat was detected closing the American ships. It was intercepted by A–6 Intruders with Harpoon missiles, which left the patrol boat dead in the water, burning, and apparently sinking.

The day ended with an A–7 Corsair high-speed anti-radiation missile (HARM) strike on Ghurdabiyah which put the site's radar out of action. Finally, at about 2200, a Libyan corvette approaching from the direction of Benghazi was hit and damaged by missiles. Meanwhile, Colonel Qaddafi was reported to have been touring Tripoli's 'people's supermarkets', declaring that his whole

AIM–9L Sidewinder on F–14 Tomcat and (below) after firing

USS *Saratoga* of the Sixth Fleet, whose aircraft intercepted the Egyptian
707 carrying the four hijackers of the Italian cruise ship *Achille Lauro*

A–7 Corsair launched from USS *Saratoga*

nation was 'racing towards the battlefield and crowding towards the war against America'.

It was probably with this exhortation in mind that a third Libyan patrol boat sailed out early on 25 March and was sunk north of the 'Line of Death' just after midnight by missiles from *Yorktown*. During that day, Ghurdabiyah (which had been repaired) was raided twice more. At about 2200, aircraft drove off a final sortie by two Libyan patrol boats.

Those events in the Gulf of Sirte had brought Libya close to open warfare with a superpower and must surely have given any rational leader pause for thought. But it was not long before US intelligence sources reported that Qaddafi was *still* fostering acts of terrorism. In April, four Americans were killed in a bomb explosion on board a TWA flight between Rome and Athens and one US serviceman was killed and fifty injured by a bomb in a West Berlin discotheque.

PRAIRIE FIRE was an ongoing contingency plan for air strikes on military targets in Libya in response to Libyan attacks causing American casualties. It was now time to light the fire again. For some days after the West Berlin discotheque bomb, EC–10 and EC–135 tankers began to fly in to air bases in southern England, to play their part in what was to be the biggest air operation mounted by the United States since the end of the Vietnam war.

The first of the sixty-six US Air Force and US Navy jets involved began to take off from bases in England at 1900 on 14 April. The main striking force of eighteen F1–11 supersonic bombers, armed with laser-guided bombs, was accompanied by three electronic-suppression USAF EF–111s, to confuse Libyan radar defences. In the Mediterranean, 150 miles off the Libyan coast, USS *Coral Sea* and *Saratoga* prepared a strike of fifteen A–6 Intruders and A–7 Corsairs.

Forbidden to fly through Spanish or French air space, the striking force had to make a lengthy detour over the Atlantic and through the Straits of Gibraltar, being refuelled in flight several times. Flying low to counter radar and surface-to-air missiles, they arrived over their targets at 2 am Libyan time on 15 April. At sea, the carriers flew off their strikes so as to co-ordinate their attack.

The F1–11s concentrated on Tripoli, the carrier planes on Benghazi. At Tripoli international airport, two Ilyushin I1–76 Candid transport aircraft were destroyed and three more damaged. There was considerable damage to buildings and casualties amongst personnel at the Azziziyah barracks compound, which included Qaddafi's headquarters, and to the combat and demolition swimmer/diver training complex at Sidi Bilal, in the Tripoli harbour area. But some bombs or rockets fell in residential areas, damaging foreign embassies and houses, and causing civilian casualties.

At Jumahiriya, Benghazi, where some of Qaddafi's personal guard were barracked and MiG spare parts were stored, warehouses and barrack buildings were damaged and MiGs in crates destroyed. The military airfield at Benina, outside Benghazi, was effectively put out of action, so that no aircraft took off in defence of the city during or immediately after the attack. Four MiG–23s, two Mil Mi–8 helicopters, and an F–27 transport were destroyed on the ground and one Mi–8, two Boeing 727s, airport buildings and vehicles were damaged.

The ground defences were slow to react, but once they began they continued to fire for some time, indeed long after the attacking aircraft had left. The shocked populations of Tripoli and Benghazi awoke to see a sky lit up by an amazing firework display of flashes and streams of tracer, with the red glow of burning buildings. One F1–11 was lost, with its two-man crew, either to anti-aircraft fire, or during the flight back.

The remaining seventeen F1–11s flew back to a reception which was almost wholly hostile except at home in the United States. Americans were unashamedly delighted, praising the British for their help and scornfully contemptuous of their critics – especially the French. The White House had more than 6,000 telephone calls in a few hours – more than it had ever received on any other single event or issue – and five out of six were congratulatory. President Reagan went on coast-to-coast television. 'Today we have done what we had to do,' he said, once again with echoes of authentic gunslinger dialogue. 'If necessary we shall do it again.'

But it seemed that where diplomatic protests, offers of negotiations and parleys, threats and ridicule had all failed, a bomb near his own tent and the death of a near-relative in the raid served to deter Colonel Qaddafi, at least for a time. At long last the United States had been able to bring just enough local force to bear upon a situation. Possibly, it could be said, President Reagan had found, or stumbled on, the art of 1980s gunboat diplomacy.

Acknowledgements

The following sources are acknowledged:

The surrender of Japan and post-war repatriation: *The Forgotten Fleet*, by John Winton (Michael Joseph, 1969)

The first jet deck landing: *Wings On My Sleeve*, by Captain Eric 'Winkle' Brown CBE, DSC, AFC, RN (Airlife Publications, 1978)

Korea: *The Sea War in Korea*, by Cdr Malcolm W. Cagle USN, and Cdr Frank A. Manson USN (United States Naval Institute, Annapolis, Maryland, 1957); *Airpower: The Decisive Force in Korea*, ed. by Colonel James T. Stewart USAF, (D. Van Nostrand Co. Inc., Princeton, New Jersey, 1957); *History of United States Naval Operations, KOREA*, by James A. Field Jr, Washington, 1962); *HMS Theseus Goes East: The Story of the Cruise of HMS Theseus to the Far East, 1950/51* (Acme Printing, Portsmouth, 1952); *Ocean Saga: HMS Ocean May 1951 to October 1953* (Hiorns and Miller, Devonport, 1954); 'British Commonwealth Naval Operations during the Korean War', Parts I–VII, *Journal of the Royal United Service Institution*, 1951–1954; *The Fleet Air Arm History*, by Lt. Cdr J. Waterman RD RNR (Retd) (Old Bond Street Publishing Co., 1975)

Suez: *Suez 1956: Operation Musketeer*, by Robert Jackson (Ian Allan, 1980); *The Naval Review*, Vol. XLV, 1957, 'The Seaborne Assault on Port Said', 'The Aircraft Carrier Aspects of Musketeer', 'The Amphibious Assault on Port Said'; 'Spreadeagle', *HMS Eagle, Ship's Magazine*, January 1957; *Air Pictorial*, August and September 1965, 'Suez 1956: A Lesson in Air Power', by V. Flintham; 'Operations in Egypt', Despatch by General Sir Charles Keightley, Supplement to *The London Gazette*, 10 September, 1957; Autobiography, by Admiral Sir Manley Power, Churchill College, Cambridge

Vietnam: *Hell In A Very Small Place; The Siege of Dien Bien Phu*, by Bernard B. Fall (Pall Mall Press, 1966); *Vietnam: A History*, by Stanley Karnow (Century Publishing, 1983); *The Naval Air War in Vietnam*, by Peter B. Mersky & Norman Polmar (Nautical and Aviation Publishing Company of America, Annapolis, Maryland, 1981)

'Jump Jet', written and produced by Brian Johnson, BBC–tv, 1980

The Falklands: HMS *Antrim*, Lt. C. J. Parry RN, Diary for 25 April 1982; HMS *Sheffield*, Captain 'Sam' Salt RN, Interview with John Winton of 18 January 1984; Lt. Cdr 'Sharkey' Ward RN and Lt. S. Thomas RN, from *Air War South Atlantic*, by Jeffrey Ethell and Alfred Price (Sidgwick & Jackson, 1983); Rear Admiral 'Sandy' Woodward, Interview with John Winton of 25 October 1982; Lt. Cdr Philippi, from *Falklands Witness of Battles*, by Jesus Romero Briasco & Salvador Mafe Huertas (Federico Domenech, Spain 1985); HMS *Broadsword*, Letter of Sub. Lt. C. M. Pickering RN to Director of Public Relations (Navy), 17 March 1983; HMS *Avenger*, from *Falklands Commando*, by Captain Hugh McManners (William Kimber, 1984)

Photo Acknowledgements

The publishers and author are grateful to the following for permission to reproduce and for supplying illustrations:

Associated Press, 184 (top); Camera Press, 109 (bottom), 168; Frederico Domenech, 146, 165; Fleet Air Arm Museum, 72, 92, 95; HMS *Ark Royal*, 131; HMS *Heron*, 10; HMS *Invincible*, 136 (top); HMS *Theseus*, 39; M. J. Hook/Shorts, 162; Robert Hunt Library, 16 (top), 20, 22, 43, 44 (bottom), 49, 96; IWM, 9, 14/15, 35, 55, 75; Rear Admiral L. E. Middleton, 76 (top); National Archives, 7; Photosource, 1, 12, 18, 28/9, 58, 60 (bottom), 65, 67, 68/9, 70, 76/7, 80, 84/5, 86, 90, 91, 99, 100, 105, 106, 109 (top), 110, 117, 119, 128, 132/3, 134, 138/9, 149, 156, 161, 166/7, 181; Popperfoto, 19, 31, 33, 34/5, 44 (top), 46/7, 52/3, 60 (top), 61, 62, 66, 116, 120, 126, 142/3, 152, 155 (inset), 178, 183; Press Association, 150, 151, 164, 170, 172; Rex Features, 82, 123, 127, 176/7,184 (bottom), 186/7, 188; Spooner/Gamma, 2/3, 140/1, 144, 155, 175; John Topham Picture Library, 16 (bottom), 87, 180; John Winton, 45, 55, 136 (bottom); US Navy, 114.

Index